D0132128

A GUIDE TO
Managing and Maintaining Your PC
LAB MANUAL

Clint Saxton, MCSE, MCT, A+

COURSE
TECHNOLOGY

ONE MAIN STREET, CAMBRIDGE, MA 02142

an International Thomson Publishing company I(T)P®

Cambridge • Albany • Bonn • Boston • Cincinnati • London • Madrid • Melbourne • Mexico City
New York • Paris • San Francisco • Singapore • Tokyo • Toronto • Washington

A Guide to Managing and Maintaining Your PC, Second Edition, Lab Manual is published by Course Technology.

Managing Editor:	Kristen Duerr
Associate Product Manager:	Lisa Ayers
Production Editor:	Ellina Beletsky
Composition House:	GEX, Inc.
Text Designer:	GEX, Inc.
Cover Designer:	Wendy J. Reifeiss
Marketing Manager:	Tracy Foley

© 1999 by Course Technology—I(T)P®

For more information contact:

Course Technology
One Main Street
Cambridge, MA 02142

ITP Europe
Berkshire House 168-173
High Holborn
London WC1IV 7AA
England

Nelson ITP Australia
102 Dodds Street
South Melbourne, 3205
Victoria, Australia

ITP Nelson Canada
1120 Birchmount Road
Scarborough, Ontario
Canada M1K 5G4

International Thomson Editores
Seneca, 53
Colonia Polanco
11560 Mexico D.F. Mexico

ITP GmbH
Königswinterer Strasse 418
53227 Bonn
Germany

ITP Asia
60 Albert Street, #15-01
Albert Complex
Singapore 189969

ITP Japan
Hirakawacho Kyowa Building, 3F
2-2-1 Hirakawacho
Chiyoda-ku, Tokyo 102
Japan

Trademarks

Course Technology and the Open Book logo are registered trademarks and CourseKits is a trademark of Course Technology. Custom Edition is a registered trademark of International Thomson Publishing.

I(T)P® The ITP logo is a registered trademark of International Thomson Publishing.

Some of the product names and company names used in this book have been used for identification purposes only and may be trademarks or registered trademarks of their respective manufacturers and sellers.

Disclaimer

Course Technology reserves the right to revise this publication and make changes from time to time in its content without notice.

ISBN 0-7600-1102-8

Printed in the United States of America

2 3 4 5 6 7 8 9 BM 02 01 00 99

BRIEF CONTENTS

TABLE OF CONTENTS

INTRODUCTION

This lab manual is designed to be used in conjunction with the second edition of A Guide to Managing and Maintaining Your PC. Inside this manual you will discover 63 exciting labs tailored to allow you simulated real-life experience through hands-on exercises. At the end of each lab exercise, a Certification Objectives section clearly outlines the A+ skills you have mastered in the previous lab. After completing all 63 lab exercises and reading the Additional A+ Coverage, you will have not only practiced each A+ objective in a hands-on environment, but also will have gained valuable Windows NT installation and configuration skills, which are vital in the quickly evolving PC industry.

The workbook was uniquely designed with you in mind and was written from the "show-me" perspective. Each lab will allow you to interact with a PC, give you the freedom to make mistakes, and most importantly, enable you to recover and LEARN from those mistakes in a safe environment. If your goal is to become an A+ certified technician, develop an understanding of operating systems, or become a PC hardware technician, this lab manual in conjunction with A Guide to Managing and Maintaining Your PC textbook will take you there!

Features

In order to ensure a successful experience for both instructors and students, this book includes the following pedagogical features:

- **Objectives**—Every lab opens with a list of learning objectives that sets the stage for students to absorb the lessons of the lab.

- **Materials Required**—This feature outlines all the materials you will need to complete the lab successfully.

- **Lab Setup & Safety Tips**—Review this quick list before beginning the lab, to ensure you are aware of any safety precautions or preliminary steps you need to take.

-  **Activity**—Each lab activity is broken down into manageable sections to ensure the student understands each step of the lab.

- **Lab Notes**—Provide the key definitions acronyms used in the body of the lab.

- **Certification Objectives**—Illustrate the A+ objectives reinforced by each lab.

- **Review Questions**—Students can test their understanding of the lab material by completing these exercises.

Acknowledgements

I would like to thank Patrick Fahey, MCSE, for both his technical expertise and friendship. A special thanks to Jamie Saxton for her continued love and support. I would also like to acknowledge all of my family for their patience and understanding. I have enjoyed working with Course Technology, and would like to send a special thanks to Lisa Ayers and Kirsten Duerr for their help in making this book a success.

I would like to thank the reviewers for their insights and valuable input. A sincere thank you to:

A. Peter Anderson
Blackhawk Technical Institute

Tom Bledsaw
ITT Technical Institute

Larry Bohn
Stream International Training

Pat Regan
Heald College

Lee Toderick
North Carolina Community College

ADDITIONAL A+ COVERAGE

ESD Electrostatic Discharge

Static Electricity

ESD stands for Electrostatic Discharge, which, by definition, means the sudden discharge of static electricity. Static electricity is everywhere, and almost all of us have experienced some form of it: it may have been from clean laundry, from touching a doorknob, or maybe even from touching a friend. All of these situations are examples of ESD. As a technician, you will come in contact with many different types of computer components, and it is your responsibility to protect the components with which you are working. Think back to the light zap on the hand from touching a doorknob, or the sound of static electricity in the clean laundry and understand that in either of these situations, had a computer component been involved, that light shock would have probably permanently damaged the component.

Types of ESD Damage

There are two types of failures caused by ESD, catastrophic failures and upset failures.

A catastrophic failure occurs when a computer component comes in contact with several thousand volts of electrostatic electricity. The component will not function properly after this encounter.

An upset failure occurs when a computer component comes in contact with several thousand volts of electrostatic electricity and begins failing sporadically.

Note that you could easily discharge 2,500 volts of static electricity to a computer component without ever seeing or feeling anything. In order for us to feel a light zap, we must be discharging at least 3,000 volts or more.

ESD Tools

Grounding straps — A grounding strap is usually an elastic wrist strap that holds a piece of metal in contact with your skin. Inside the wrist strap, a resistor is connected on one side to the metal against your skin, and on the other side, the resistor is connected to a wire. This wire is your grounding wire and, when properly used, should be attached to something that is equal to ground or 0 volts. When working with computer components at a customer's desk, the grounding strap wire is commonly attached to the computer chassis.

Grounding mats — Grounding mats are normally made of rubber or specially coated plastic and are designed to maintain charge equal to ground. A grounding mat has a wire that is embedded into the mat that should also be attached to ground.

Smocks — A smock is something like a jacket. Smocks are specially designed overcoats used to minimize static electricity produced on your clothing. Smocks are most commonly used in computer component assembly or repair lines.

Grounding foot straps — Grounding foot straps serve the same purpose as the grounding strap. A grounding foot strap has metal on the bottom and is worn over shoes. In order for grounding foot straps to work effectively, you must be standing up and the metal must touch a non-carpeted surface. Grounding foot straps are usually used in combination with other grounding tools.

Static shielded bags (ESD bags) — An ESD or static shielded bag is made of silver material and bears an industry-recognized marking. When using a static shielded bag, be sure to place the component completely inside the bag and fold the top over and tape it. This is the only way to ensure proper ESD protection.

ESD stations — An ESD safe area is sometimes referred to as an ESD station. ESD stations most commonly consist of a non-conductive workbench area. Almost all ESD stations have a grounding mat, an area to plug in your grounding strap, and some sort of a grounding strap testing device. *Note*: It is important to test grounding straps on a daily basis.

Certification Objectives

Core A+ Objectives

Objective	Chapters	Page Numbers
3.5 Identify ESD (Electrostatic Discharge) precautions and procedures, including the use of ESD protection devices. Content may include the following:		
What ESD can do, how it may be apparent, or hidden	Introduction, 2, 3	xxiv, 73, 130
Common ESD protection devices	Introduction, 3, 6, 7	xxiv, 130, 264, 335-336
Situations that could present a danger or hazard	2, 3, 7, 13	73, 130, 335, 690

Consumables and Their Disposal

All laser printers require consumable supplies. The replacement interval for a specific consumable depends on the brand of printer, the type of consumable supply needed, and the usage of the printer. With personal and office printers, the consumables can be very expensive in proportion to the purchase price of the printer itself. Consumers who perform a lot of printing may spend as much in one year on consumables as the original cost of the printer. Therefore, when choosing a printer, it is very important to consider the type of consumables it requires, the frequency of replacement, and the cost of each consumable.

Estimated Printer Life

Like all mechanical devices, a printer will wear out, and most printers are built to provide a specific life when used under a particular set of conditions.

Workgroup printers vary in their longevity—the smallest workgroup printers will probably last only 500,000 pages. The more industrial models, with regular preventive maintenance, can survive for millions of pages.

Production printers are generally designed to last as long as possible. Large production printers can run almost continuously and produce more than half a million prints a week, so with regular maintenance, some production printers are likely to exceed 250 million prints before they will need to be replaced.

Most personal printers are built to produce between 100,000 and 150,000 pages, although some of the more inexpensive models are only expected to survive 30,000 pages (100 pages per week, for several years).

What Happens to Recycled Printer Cartridges

Printer cartridges usually need to be replaced before other printer parts have finished their useful life. To reuse the mechanical elements in a print cartridge, some suppliers recycle them and refill them with toner. The degree of recycling varies considerably. There are many small companies that will simply test the print cartridge and refill it. Others, including some printer manufacturers, completely rebuild the print cartridge. In this situation, most will provide a warranty for the cartridge.

Generally, you should avoid refilled cartridges unless the price is so advantageous that it compensates for the risk of poor print quality associated with them. While most refurbishing companies do their best to test for good quality, the photoreceptor surface on a refilled ink cartridge may not be as good as it is on a new cartridge. Note also that the mechanical elements (gearwheels, drive belts, etc.) may be worn, which will lead to premature failure.

Printer cartridges that have actually been rebuilt can usually be expected to perform like new cartridges. The labor cost of disassembling, cleaning, checking, and rebuilding a cartridge is nearly equal to the cost of making a new cartridge. Therefore the price of a rebuilt cartridge is only slightly less than that of a new cartridge.

Printer Cartridge Disposal

Consumers are responsible for the proper disposal of printer cartridges. It is recommended that consumers recycle their printer cartridges so that the cartridge may be rejuvenated using one of the previously discussed methods. As a rule of thumb, disposal of computer equipment in the private sector is the consumer's responsibility and it is acceptable for consumers to dispose of computer equipment using their standard trash disposal methods. However, businesses are required to abide by a set of state and federal laws which outlines what methods should be used for computer component disposal. You will need to check the laws of the state where your business operates.

Certification Objectives

Core A+ Objectives

Objective	Chapters	Page Numbers
3.4 Identify items that require special disposal procedures that comply with environmental guidelines. Content may include the following:		
Toner kits/cartridges	Student Lab Manual	N/A
Computers	Check local state law for proper disposal	N/A
Chemical solvents and cans	Check local state law for proper disposal	N/A
CRTs	Check local state law for proper disposal	N/A
MSDS (Material Safety Data Sheet)	Check local state law for proper disposal	N/A

Battery Disposal Guide

This section outlines the requirements most businesses must follow for battery disposal. Consumers are not required to follow these rules and are allowed to dispose of batteries using their normal trash disposal method. Note that not all of these batteries are used in the computer industry, but should still be discussed or made available to the students.

Alkaline Batteries

Alkaline batteries include AAA, AA, A, C, D and 9-volt.

Disposal: Normal trash

Lead Acid Batteries

Lead acid batteries are found in cars, trucks, and most other vehicles.

Disposal: Do *not* place in normal trash. Exchange old battery for new one at dealer.

Button Batteries

Button batteries are found in watches, calculators, cameras, and other small equipment. They can contain silver oxide, mercury, lithium, or cadmium. These materials are considered hazardous waste. Contents can be determined by reading original battery packaging.

Disposal: Do *not* place in normal trash. Return to dealer for recycling. Button batteries can only be recycled if they are segregated on the basis of metal content. To facilitate this, try to get into the habit of keeping the original packaging for reference once the battery is spent.

Lithium Batteries

Lithium batteries are found in some electronic equipment. See original packaging for content information.

Disposal: Do *not* place in normal trash. Return to the dealer for recycling. Keep lithium batteries separate from other batteries when collecting.

Nickel Cadmium (NiCad) Batteries

NiCad batteries are found in items including medical equipment, pagers, and cellular telephones. Check original packaging for content information.

Disposal: Do *not* place in normal trash. Return to the dealer for recycling. Keep NiCad batteries separate from other batteries when collecting.

Certification Objectives

Core A+ Objectives

Objective	Chapters	Page Numbers
3.4 Identify items that require special disposal procedures that comply with environmental guidelines. Content may include the following:		
Batteries	Student Lab Manual	N/A
Computers	Check local state law for proper disposal	N/A
Chemical solvents and cans	Check local state law for proper disposal	N/A
CRTs	Check local state law for proper disposal	N/A
MSDS (Material Safety Data Sheet)	Check local state law for proper disposal	N/A

Notebook Computers

AC adapter — At the time of purchase, most notebooks include one AC adapter. The purpose of the AC adapter is to act as the power supply for the notebook by converting AC current to DC current. *Warning:* Not all notebooks require the same amount of DC voltage, therefore it is important that you use the correct AC adapter for your notebook.

Battery pack — At the time of purchase, most notebook computers include one battery pack. This is used when the notebook is not powered through the AC adapter. Note that most notebooks have the ability to charge their battery pack while being powered by the AC adapter.

Floppy drive — At the time of purchase, most notebook computers include a floppy drive. A floppy drive's location and design varies depending on the vendor of the notebook.

CD-ROM — Although CD-ROMs for notebooks are quickly becoming standard equipment, they are not always sold with a notebook computer as part of the basic package. This means that you may have to purchase the CD-ROM separately.

Infrared (IR) — This feature has quickly become a standard among notebook computers and is almost always included at the time of purchase. Note that often, notebooks have the option to use either infrared or a COM port, but normally not both. This means that you would probably have to disable one of the COM ports to enable infrared.

Liquid Crystal Display (LCD) — Almost all notebook computers use an LCD display for their screen. Some of the features to look for in an LCD are size, picture quality, and ease of configuration. *Warning:* Some LCDs require special drivers that must be set to a particular resolution in order to function properly.

Docking station — A docking station is a "shell" into which a notebook can be automatically connected and configured. When a notebook is docked, the docking station emulates the external ports of the notebook. The docking station can then be attached to external devices such as a monitor, keyboard, mouse, and COM devices.

Port replicator — A port replicator serves the same purpose as a docking station. The difference is that most port replicators do not contain as many external ports as docking stations.

All about PC Cards

Type I — These PC cards can be up to 3.3mm thick and are most commonly used as RAM expansions cards for notebook computers.

Type II — These cards can be up to 5.5mm thick and are primarily used for notebook modems.

Type III — These PC cards can be up to 10.5mm thick and are large enough to accommodate a portable disk drive.

Certification Objectives

Core A+ Objectives

Objective	Chapters	Page Numbers
6.1 Identify the unique components of portable systems and their unique problems. Content may include the following:		
Battery	Student Lab Manual	N/A
AC adapter	Student Lab Manual	N/A
Docking stations	8	406
Hard Drive	8	406
Types I, II, III cards	8	406-407
Network cards	8	406-407
Memory	8	406, 434

The LCD Troubleshooting Guide

The video does not turn on

Warranties for notebook computers are often dependnet upon the case not being opened. Therefore, the connections of the LCD display are unavailable and should not be tampered with. To test a system with no video, first be sure it is turned on. Second, try connecting an external monitor using the external VGA port on the notebook.

The screen is too dark

Most LCDs have adjustment controls which are used to manage the brightness and contrast of the display. Refer to the user manual that came with the notebook for details about your computer.

The display is always in VGA mode

This normally occurs when the wrong driver is installed or there is no driver configured for the display. Note that because most notebook computers require OEM drivers, you must check the user manual included with the notebook for correct driver configurations.

The screen periodically displays odd lines, jumps, shakes, or gets fuzzy

This could be caused by environmental distortion. Electrical interference from devices such as radios, televisions, and microwave ovens can cause the monitor to display odd lines, jump, or shake. Note that interference can also make the display appear blurry or fuzzy.

Nothing will turn on: Is my monitor broken?

This can be caused by any number of things, but most likely, the monitor is not broken. One of the easiest things a user can do to attempt to reset or reboot their system is to remove the battery and unplug the computer. Next, plug in the computer without the battery and press the reset button.

Certification Objectives

Core A+ Objectives

Objective	Chapters	Page Numbers
6.1 Identify the unique components of portable systems and their unique problems. Content may include the following:		
LCD	Lab Manual	N/A

A+ Objective Notes

Due to the similarities between upgrading and installing Windows 95, the following A+ Objective was not directly addressed. However, installing Windows 95 from within a DOS environment is addressed in Lab Exercise 11.3, and upgrading from Windows 3.1 to Windows NT is addressed in Lab 12.1.

Objective	Chapters	Page Numbers
3.2 Identify steps to perform an operating system upgrade. Content may include the following:		
Upgrading from Win 3.x to Win95	11	559

CHAPTER ONE

HOW COMPUTERS WORK - AN OVERVIEW

LABS INCLUDED IN THIS CHAPTER

LAB 1.1 COMPONENTS OF A PERSONAL COMPUTER SYSTEM

LAB 1.2 OPERATING A DOS-BASED PC

LAB 1.3 OPERATING A WINDOWS 3.x-BASED PC

LAB 1.4 OPERATING A WINDOWS 95-BASED PC

LAB 1.1   COMPONENTS OF A PERSONAL COMPUTER SYSTEM

Objective

The objective of this lab is to introduce you to the components of a personal computer (PC) system, which include: monitor, keyboard, mouse, printer, printer cable, power cables, and system unit. After completing this lab exercise you will be able to:

- Identify the various components of a PC system.

- Describe the functionality of the various PC system components.

- Attach each of the most commonly used devices.

- Properly perform basic cleaning and maintenance procedures for each of the most commonly used PC components.

Materials Required

This lab will require one complete lab workstation for every four students. The lab workstations should meet the following requirements:

- 486 or better
- At least 4MB of RAM
- 540MB or larger hard drive

Labels for each group of students

Paper towels for each group of students

At least two spray bottles filled with a cleaning solution of either water and ammonia or water and liquid soap

One demonstration PC with each of the following components properly attached and labeled:

- Monitor
- Keyboard
- Mouse
- Printer
- Printer cable
- Power cables
- System unit

 ### Lab Setup & Safety Tips

- Each group of students should have all of the following PC components unattached:

- Monitor
- Keyboard
- Mouse
- Power cables
- System unit

ACTIVITY

Attaching your lab workstation's devices

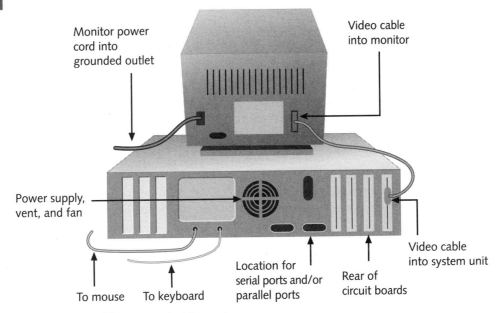

Monitor power cord into grounded outlet

Video cable into monitor

Power supply, vent, and fan

To mouse   To keyboard

Location for serial ports and/or parallel ports

Rear of circuit boards

Video cable into system unit

Figure 1-1   Cables connected to ports

1. Observe the configuration of your instructor's demonstration PC.

2. Write down the name and functionality of each device labeled on your instructor's demonstration PC.

_____

_____

_____

_____

3. Attach your lab workstation's components in the same manner as your instructor's demonstration PC.

4. Power on your lab workstation to verify that each component has been properly connected.

5. After your instructor has verified proper operation, power down your system.

Cleaning your mouse

1. Turn the mouse upside down.

2. Locate and remove the cover of the mouse ball.

3. Remove the mouse ball.

4. Inside the housing of the mouse ball, you will find several rollers. Clear these rollers of debris.

5. After clearing any debris that might be located on the rollers, replace the mouse ball and cover.

Cleaning your monitor

1. Using a paper towel lightly spray the towel with water or a manufacturer recommended cleaning solution from a spray bottle (never spray anything directly on the screen of your monitor).

2. Gently wipe the entire screen using the slightly damp paper towel.

Cleaning your keyboard

Keyboards are generally cleaned by placing them in an automatic dishwasher. When using this method be sure to allow the keyboard to completely dry before attempting to use it again. Note: It is not always necessary to wash a keyboard; many times simply turning over the keyboard and shaking it will allow dust and other debris to fall out.

Clearing a stuck key

Most keyboards are designed to allow the keys to be removed by gently pulling or prying the key upwards. This procedure is most commonly used when debris has become jammed underneath a particular key.

Cleaning the exterior case of the system unit

1. Lightly spray a paper towel with water or a manufacturer recommended cleaning solution from a spray bottle (never spray anything directly on the exterior of your system unit case).

2. Gently wipe the entire case using the slightly damp paper towel.

Lab Notes

Although every PC has different peripherals and types of devices, there are several components that all PCs require. The following is a list of the components required by any PC:

- Monitor
- Keyboard
- Mouse
- Power cables
- System unit

CERTIFICATION OBJECTIVES

Table 1-1   Core A+ objectives

Objective	Chapters	Page Numbers
1.1 Identify basic terms, concepts, and functions of system modules, including how each module should work during normal operation. Examples of concepts and modules:		
Monitor	1, 4	2, 175
1.2 Identify basic procedures for adding and removing field replaceable modules. Examples of modules:		
Monitor	14	748
3.1 Identify the purpose of various types of preventive maintenance products and procedures, and when to use/perform them. Content may include the following:		
Liquid cleaning compounds	4	181
Types of materials to clean contacts and connections	4, 17	181, 899
Manufacturer guidelines	17	898, 899

REVIEW QUESTIONS

Circle True or False.

1. A monitor requires one cord and one cable to function properly. True / False

2. Most keyboards have their own power source. True / False

3. The mouse and keyboard connections are interchangeable. True / False

4. How many cables and cords are connected to the system unit, and which devices are they connected to?

   _____

   _____

   _____

   _____

   _____

5. You are employed as a desktop PC support technician at the PC Store. Matt, one of your customers, has called you with a problem. He explains that he just finished moving his PC and reconnecting all of the cables, but now he is getting error messages and both the keyboard and mouse won't work. What is the most likely cause of Matt's problem?

   _____

   _____

   _____

   _____

   _____

6. Another customer, Judy, has also just finished moving her PC, but now the monitor screen won't show a picture. She explains that the power light for the monitor is turned on and that the system unit power light is on also. Which cables would you ask Judy to check first?

   _____

   _____

   _____

   _____

   _____

7. Describe how to clean a mouse.

   _____

   _____

   _____

   _____

LAB 1.2 OPERATING A DOS-BASED PC

Objective

The objective of this lab exercise is to provide you with the experience of creating both files and directories in the DOS environment. After completing this lab exercise you will be able to:

- Start a DOS computer.
- Start a DOS application.
- Create a DOS system disk.
- Create a directory.
- Create and save a text file.
- Describe the purpose of a system disk.
- Properly shut down your DOS lab workstation.

Materials Required

One MS-DOS lab workstation for every three students. The lab workstations should meet the following requirements:

- 486 or better
- At least 4MB of RAM
- 540MB or larger hard drive

One unformatted floppy disk for each lab workstation

Lab Setup & Safety Tips

- This lab assumes that the DOS operating system is installed in a directory called DOS.
- Each lab workstation should have MS-DOS 5.0 or greater installed and functioning properly.
- After completing this lab exercise, be sure to keep your system disk in a safe place; it will be needed in future labs.

ACTIVITY

Creating a DOS system disk

1. Power on your lab workstation, and allow it to boot into the DOS environment.
2. Place the blank unformatted disk in drive A.
3. At the C prompt, type **SYS C: A:**.
4. Press **Enter**.
5. Type **CD DOS** and press **Enter**.
6. Type **COPY FDISK A:** and press **Enter**.
7. Type **COPY FORMAT A:** and press **Enter**.
8. Type **COPY SCANDISK A:** and press **Enter**.
9. Type **COPY DEFRAG A:** and press **Enter**.

Understanding a DOS system disk

1. Place the system disk in drive A.

2. Turn on the PC.

3. Record the results.

_____

4. Turn off the PC.

5. Place the unformatted disk in drive A.

6. Turn on the PC.

7. Record the results.

_____

8. Turn off the PC.

9. Remove the floppy disk from drive A.

Creating a file using DOS EDIT

1. Turn on the PC, and allow it to boot into the DOS environment.

2. Type **EDIT** at the C prompt.

3. Type the following text in the Edit program, **This is a test file**.

4. Hold down the Alt key and at the same time press the letter "F".

5. Use the down arrow [↓] to select **Save As** from the File menu.

6. At the top of the Save As dialog box, locate the **File Name** section.

7. Type the following filename, **C:\Test.txt**.

8. Press **Enter** on the keyboard.

9. Hold down the Alt key and at the same time press the letter "F".

10. Use the down arrow [↓] to select **Exit** from the File menu.

Creating a directory

1. At the C prompt, type the following, **MD C:\LAB1.2** and press **Enter**. Your lab workstation should respond by returning you to a C prompt.

Lab Notes

EDIT – The Edit program is a DOS text editor that is used to create and modify text files in the DOS environment.

DOS system disk – A DOS system disk is a bootable disk that allows a PC to be booted using a minimal amount of DOS system files.

MD – The MD, or Make Directory command, is used to create a directory in the DOS environment.

How do I shut down DOS? – DOS is one of the simplest operating systems to shut down; you simply power off the PC.

CERTIFICATION OBJECTIVES

Table 1-2   DOS/Windows A+ objectives

Objective	Chapters	Page Numbers
1.2 Identify ways to navigate the operating system and how to get to needed technical information. Content may include the following:		
Procedures (e.g., menu or icon -driven) for navigating through DOS to perform such things as locating, accessing, and retrieving information	5	208-214
3.3 Identify the basic system boot sequences for DOS, Windows 3.x, and Windows 95, and alternative ways to boot the system software. Content may include the following:		
Booting a system from floppy, hard drive	2	66, 70
Strategies to be used	11	527, 551

REVIEW QUESTIONS

Circle True or False.

1. When booting an MS-DOS computer, you must always have a system disk in drive A. True / False

2. Before powering off a DOS system, you should first execute the SHUTDOWN DOS command. True / False

3. Only black disks can be used as system disks. True / False

4. The Edit program can be used to create DOS system disks. True / False

5. Describe the most obvious difference between a DOS system disk and other formatted disks.

   _____

   _____

   _____

   _____

   _____

6. You are working as a PC desktop support technician at the Fun Job Corporation. Kyle, one of your customers, just rebooted his PC after copying some files from a disk to his hard drive. Kyle says that he is receiving the error message, "Non-system disk or disk error," and it just keeps repeating that error no matter what he does. Describe what the problem is and how Kyle should go about resolving the problem.

   _____

   _____

   _____

   _____

   _____

LAB 1.3   OPERATING A WINDOWS 3.x-BASED PC

Objective

The objective of this lab exercise is to provide you with the ability to operate and navigate in the Windows 3.x environment. After completing this lab exercise, you will be able to:

- Start a Windows 3.x-based computer.

- Start an application on a Windows 3.x-based computer.

- Create and save a text file in the Windows 3.x environment.

- Create a directory using File Manager.

- Shut down your Windows 3.x lab workstation.

Materials Required

One Windows 3.x lab workstation for every three students. The lab workstation should meet the following requirements:

- 486 or better
- At least 4MB of RAM
- 540MB or larger hard drive

Lab Setup & Safety Tips

- Each lab workstation should have Window 3.x installed and functioning properly.

ACTIVITY

Creating a text file in Windows 3.x

1. Power on the lab workstation, and allow it to boot into the Windows environment.

2. In Program Manager, double-click the **Accessories** group icon.

3. Double-click the **Notepad** program icon.

4. In the Notepad window, type **This a test file**.

5. In the upper-left corner of the Notepad window, click the **File** menu, and then click **Save As**.

6. In the File Name section of the Save As dialog box, type **test.txt**.

7. Click the **Save** button.

8. In the Notepad window, click **File**, and then click **Exit**.

Creating a directory

1. Locate the Main group in the **Program Manager** window.

2. Double-click **Main**.

3. Double-click **File Manager**.

4. Single-click your **drive C** icon to highlight it.

5. Click the **File** menu in the upper-left corner of the File Manager window.

6. Select **Create Directory** from the File menu.

7. Type **LAB1.3** and press **Enter**.

8. Verify that the directory was created by looking on your drive C for a yellow folder called LAB1.3.

Shutting down Windows 3.x

1. In the Program Manager window, click the **File** menu, and then click **Exit**.

2. Click the **Yes** button when prompted.

3. When Windows has exited to DOS, power off the lab workstation.

Lab Notes

Notepad – Notepad is the Windows 3.x equivalent of the DOS Edit program. It is a simple text editor you can use to create and modify text files.

File Manager – File Manager is a Windows based utility designed to simplify file and directory management.

CERTIFICATION OBJECTIVES

Table 1-3   DOS/Windows A+ objectives

Objective	Chapters	Page Numbers
1.1 Identify the operating system's functions, structure, and major system files. Content may include the following:		
Functions of DOS, Windows 3.x and Windows 95	1	20-22
1.2 Identify ways to navigate the operating system and how to get to needed technical information. Content may include the following:		
Procedures for navigating through the Windows 3.x/Windows 95 operating system, accessing, and retrieving information	5	214-219

REVIEW QUESTIONS

Circle True or False.

1. You can use either Windows or DOS to create a directory. True / False

2. To create a directory in Windows 3.x, you can use the Notepad program. True / False

3. Notepad is the equivalent of the DOS command MD. True / False

4. Where is the Notepad icon found by default in Windows 3.1?

_____

_____

_____

_____

5. Rick is trying to locate an important document that he misplaced. He wants to use File Manager to locate the document but can't remember how to start it. List the instructions you would give Rick to help him start File Manager.

_____

_____

_____

_____

_____

6. Tom has written a quick letter in Notepad. He now wants to save the letter to drive C. Describe how Tom should go about saving his letter from within Notepad.

_____

_____

_____

_____

_____

LAB 1.4 OPERATING A WINDOWS 95-BASED PC

Objective

The objective of this lab exercise is to provide you with the ability to operate and navigate in the Windows 95 environment. After completing this lab exercise, you will be able to:

- Start a Windows 95 computer.
- Start an application within Windows 95.
- Create and save a text file in the Windows 95 environment.
- Create a directory using the Windows Explorer.
- Shut down your Windows 95 lab workstation.

Materials Required

One Windows 95 lab workstation for every three students. The lab workstations should meet the following requirements:

- 486 or better
- At least 8MB of RAM
- 540MB or larger hard drive
- Windows 95

Lab Setup & Safety Tips

- Each lab workstation should have Windows 95 installed and functioning properly.

ACTIVITY

Creating a text file in Windows 95

1. Power on the lab workstation and allow it to boot into the Windows environment.
2. Click the **Start** button.
3. Point to **Programs**, and then click **Accessories**.
4. Click **Notepad**.
5. In the Notepad window, type **this is a Windows 95 test file**.
6. In the upper-left corner of the Notepad window, click the **File** menu, and then click **Save As**.
7. In the File Name section of the Save As dialog box, type **test.txt**.
8. Click the **Save** button.
9. In the Notepad window, click **File**, and then click **Exit**.

Creating a folder (directory)

1. Click the **Start** button.
2. Point to **Programs**.
3. Click **Windows Explorer**.
4. Click your **drive C** icon to highlight it.
5. Click the **File** menu in the upper-left corner of the Windows Explorer.

6. Point to **New** and click **Folder**.

7. Type **LAB1.4** and press **Enter**.

8. Verify that the directory was created by looking on your drive C for a yellow folder called LAB1.4.

Shutting down Windows 95

1. Click the **Start** button.

2. Click **Shut Down**.

3. Select the **Shut Down the computer?** option in the Shut Down Windows dialog box, and then click the **Yes** button.

4. Wait for Windows to completely shut down and tell you that it is safe to turn off your computer.

Lab Notes

Notepad – Notepad is the Windows 95 equivalent of the DOS Edit program. It is simply a text editor you can use to create and modify text files.

Windows Explorer – The Windows Explorer is a Windows-based utility designed to simplify file and directory management. It is the Windows 95 equivalent of File Manager.

What is the difference between a folder and a directory? – A folder and a directory are the same thing. The difference lies in the operating system you are using. In the DOS environment, the correct term is directory, whereas in the Windows 95 environment the term is folder.

CERTIFICATION OBJECTIVES

Table 1-4   DOS/Windows A+ objectives

Objective	Chapters	Page Numbers
1.2 Identify ways to navigate the operating system and how to get to needed technical information. Content may include the following:		
Procedures for navigating through the Windows 3.x/Windows 95 operating system, accessing, and retrieving information	5	214-219

REVIEW QUESTIONS

Circle True or False.

1. The Notepad program in Windows 95 can be found in the Accessories group. True / False

2. Notepad can be used to write short text files. True / False

3. Using Notepad you can only create and manipulate one text document at a time. True / False

4. Where can the Accessories group be found in the Windows 95 environment?

_____

_____

_____

_____

_____

5. The Windows Explorer is a replacement for the Windows 3.x _____ utility.

6. You are employed at the Happy Day Corporation. Bill, the manager of your department, has a new laptop with Windows 95. He is new to the Windows 95 environment and is trying to shut down his computer. List the instructions you would give Bill to properly shut down his Windows 95 laptop.

_____

_____

_____

_____

_____

7. Two days later you are chatting with Bill and he asks you where to find File Manager on his laptop. Write your answer to Bill's question below.

_____

_____

_____

_____

_____

How Software and Hardware Work Together

LABS INCLUDED IN THIS CHAPTER

LAB 2.1 CMOS MANIPULATION

LAB 2.2 IRQ AND DMA MANAGEMENT

LAB 2.3 I/O MANAGEMENT

LAB 2.4 THE BOOT PROCESS

Lab 2.1 CMOS Manipulation

Objective

The objective of this lab is to familiarize you with the operation of your lab workstation's CMOS setup program. After completing this lab exercise, you will be able to:

- Customize the operation and configuration of a PC utilizing the CMOS setup program.

Materials Required

One Windows 95 lab workstation for every four students. The lab workstations should meet the following requirements:

- 486 or better
- At least 8MB of RAM
- 540MB or larger hard drive

Lab Setup & Safety Tips

- Because there are so many different types of setup programs, it is recommended that you ask for some basic tips from your instructor before proceeding.

Activity

Creating a System Configuration Worksheet

A System Configuration Worksheet is a spreadsheet or some sort of document that contains all of your workstation's CMOS configuration parameters. Use the sections below to develop your own System Configuration Worksheet for your lab workstation.

For each of the following system components, record the information currently saved in your lab workstation's CMOS.

CPU _____

Memory _____

IDE 1 _____

IDE 2 _____

IDE 3 _____

IDE 4 _____

SCSI _____

_____

_____

Serial 1 _____

Serial 2 _____

LPT 1 _____

Network card _____

Changing CMOS values

1. Review the System Configuration Worksheet provided for your computer.

2. Start your PC.

3. Following the instructions provided on your screen, enter the setup program.

4. Change the DATE for your computer to today's date, in the year 2000.

5. Change the Hard Disk Drive configuration to NONE.

6. Save your changes.

7. Shut down your computer, and allow it to reboot.

8. Observe the changes in the startup sequence.

9. Enter the setup program.

10. Reconfigure your hard drive to match the parameters of your System Configuration Worksheet.

11. Activate the Power Management on your PC.

12. Assign the password of LAB in all capital letters to your system setup program.

13. Save your changes.

14. Shut down your computer and allow it to reboot.

15. Observe the changes in the startup sequence.

Restoring your lab workstation using the System Configuration Worksheet

1. Type the system startup password.

2. Enter the setup program.

3. Disable the system startup password.

4. Referring to the System Configuration Worksheet, verify that all CMOS settings are back to their original configuration.

Lab Notes

How do I flash the CMOS? – The process of flashing a computer's CMOS is somewhat dangerous for the computer. If the CMOS is flashed with the incorrect BIOS update or is interrupted during the flash, the data on the EEPROM chip could be lost or corrupted and render the system BIOS useless. For this reason there is not a lab exercise allowing you to flash a workstation's BIOS.

CERTIFICATION OBJECTIVES

Table 2-1   Core A+ objectives

Objective	Chapters	Page Numbers
1.1 Identify basic terms, concepts, and functions of system modules, including how each module should work during normal operation. Examples of concepts and modules:		
BIOS	1, 2, 3	6, 56, 61, 99-105
CMOS	1, 2, 3	7, 51-53, 120
1.9 Identify procedures for upgrading BIOS.		
Upgrade system BIOS (flash or replace)	3, 5, 6	102, 105, 200-201, 267
2.1 Identify common symptoms and problems associated with each module and how to troubleshoot and isolate the problems. Content may include the following:		
BIOS	2, 3	56, 101-102
POST audible/visual error codes	App. A	A1
4.4 Identify the purpose of CMOS (Complementary Metal-Oxide Semiconductor), what it contains and how to change its basic parameters. Example Basic CMOS Settings:		
printer parallel port - Uni., bi-directional, disable/enable, ECP, EPP	14	748-751
com/serial port – memory address, interrupt request, disable	1, 3	7, 51, 120-121
hard drive - size and drive type	1, 3	7, 120-121
floppy drive – enable/disable drive or boot, speed, density	1, 3	7, 120-121
memory - parity, non-parity	3	120-121
date/time	2, 3	53, 120-121
passwords	2, 3	52, 120-121

REVIEW QUESTIONS

Circle True or False.

1. A System Configuration Worksheet is used to record your operating system's configuration.
   True / False

2. The system time and date are always configured through the CMOS SETUP program.
   True / False

3. Always record your CMOS settings before making changes. True / False

4. Describe some of the dangers of flashing a BIOS.

   _____

   _____

   _____

   _____

   _____

5. You are employed at the Yesterday Company as a desktop PC support technician. Karl, a coworker, is adding a hard drive to a computer. Karl has verified that the hard drive is properly connected and powered, but the computer still won't recognize the drive. What recommendations can you give Karl?

_____

_____

_____

_____

_____

6. You just finished installing 32MB of RAM into Umair's computer for him. You now want to verify that Umair's computer is recognizing all 32MB of RAM. Describe below how you could verify the memory configuration on Umair's computer.

_____

_____

_____

_____

_____

LAB 2.2 IRQ AND DMA MANAGEMENT

Objective

The objective of this lab is to provide you with the necessary experience of viewing currently installed device drivers, modifying their IRQ, DMA and I/O address settings and developing a general understanding of resource allocations. After completing this lab exercise, you will be able to:

- List examples of standard IRQ, DMA, and I/O usage.

- Explain how to determine which IRQ, DMA, and I/O channels and addresses are being utilized.

- Explain how to modify IRQ, DMA, and I/O address settings to resolve resource conflicts.

- Identify installed device drivers in the Windows 95 environment.

Materials Required

One Windows 95 lab workstation for every four students. The lab workstations should meet the following requirements:

- 486 or better
- At least 8MB of RAM
- 540MB or larger hard drive

Lab Setup & Safety Tips

- Each lab workstation should have Windows 95 installed and functioning properly.

ACTIVITY

Recording your lab workstation's IRQ settings

1. Start your lab workstation, and allow it to boot into Windows 95.

2. Click the **Start** button.

3. Point to **Settings**.

4. Click **Control Panel**.

5. Double-click the **System** icon.

6. Click the **Device Manager** tab.

7. Click the **Properties** button.

8. Record the device name for each of the following IRQs "on".

   IRQ 00 _____

   IRQ 01 _____

   IRQ 02 _____

   IRQ 03 _____

   IRQ 04 _____

   IRQ 05 _____

   IRQ 06 _____

   IRQ 07 _____

IRQ 08 _____

IRQ 09 _____

IRQ 10 _____

IRQ 11 _____

IRQ 12 _____

IRQ 13 _____

IRQ 14 _____

IRQ 15 _____

Recording your lab workstation's DMA settings

1. Start your lab workstation, and allow it to boot into Windows 95.

2. Click the **Start** button.

3. Point to **Settings**.

4. Click **Control Panel**.

5. Double-click on the **System** icon.

6. Click the **Device Manager** tab.

7. Click the **Properties** button.

8. Click the **Direct Memory Access (DMA)** option button.

9. Record the device name for each of the following DMA channels.

DMA 01 _____

DMA 02 _____

DMA 03 _____

DMA 04_____

Lab Notes

Device Manager – Device Manager is a Windows 95 program that you can use to view all of the currently installed device drivers and their resource configuration.

What is an IRQ? – An IRQ is a number that is assigned to a device and is used to signal the CPU for servicing.

What is a DMA? – A DMA controller chip is a chip that resides on the systemboard and provides channels that a device may use to send data directly to memory, bypassing the CPU.

CERTIFICATION OBJECTIVES

Table 2-2   Core A+ objectives

Objective	Chapters	Page Numbers
1.3 Identify available IRQs, DMA's, and I/O addresses and procedures for configuring them for device installation, including identifying switch and jumper settings. Content may include the following:		
Standard IRQ settings	3	123

Table 2-3   DOS/Windows A+ objectives

Objective	Chapters	Page Numbers
1.2 Identify ways to navigate the operating system and how to get to needed technical information. Content may include the following:		
Procedures for navigating through the Windows 3.x/ Windows 95 operating system, accessing, and retrieving information	5	214-219

REVIEW QUESTIONS

Circle True or False.

1. The Device Manager utility can be used to view all of the DMA channels and the devices currently configured to use them. True / False

2. Device Manager is located on the Control Panel and accessed through the Add New Hardware icon. True / False

3. IRQ stand for internal response question. True / False

4. DMA stands for direct memory access True / False

5. You are employed as a hardware technician at Crunchy Com Corporation. One of your coworkers, Todd, just finished installing a modem into a customer's computer. Unfortunately, the modem doesn't seem to be functioning properly. Todd believes there is a resource conflict between the modem and another device. Todd asks you for help because he is new to the Windows 95 environment. Write the steps you would take to help Todd discover a resource conflict.

   _____

   _____

   _____

   _____

   _____

6. Referring to your list of IRQs, which device is IRQ 15 normally reserved for?

   _____

   _____

   _____

   _____

   _____

2

LAB 2.3 I/O MANAGEMENT

Objective

The objective of this lab is to provide you with experience in the management of I/O addresses, and in the resolution of conflicts between I/O addresses. After completing this lab exercise, you will be able to:

- Explain the importance of unique I/O addresses.

- Determine which I/O addresses are being utilized.

- Identify and resolve an I/O address conflict.

- Install a network interface card.

Materials Required

One Windows 95 lab workstation for every four students. The lab workstations should meet the following requirements:

- 486 or better
- At least 8MB of RAM
- 540MB or larger hard drive

One network interface card that will be used to create a conflict with an assigned I/O address

One ESD mat for each lab workstation

Grounding straps for each student

The necessary tools for removing the lab workstation's case and adding a network interface card

One network interface card per a lab workstation. (Note: This card should not be installed at the beginning of the lab exercise.)

Documentation for the network interface card, including jumper settings

Lab Setup & Safety Tips

- Each lab workstation should have Windows 95 installed and functioning properly.

- Each group of students should have one network interface card in an ESD safe bag and documentation describing the proper jumper settings for the card.

- Always verify that the power cord is removed from the PC before touching components inside the computer's case.

ACTIVITY

Creating the I/O address conflict

Your instructor will tell you at which I/O address you will be creating a conflict.

1. Start your lab workstation, and allow it to boot into Windows 95.

2. Click the **Start** button.

3. Point to **Settings**.

4. Click **Control Panel**.

5. Double-click the **System** icon.

6. Click the **Device Manager** tab.

7. Click the **Properties** button.

8. Click the **I/O (Input/Output)** option button.

9. Observe the current device configurations of the predetermined I/O address.

10. Click the **Cancel** button.

11. Close Device Manager and shut down Windows.

12. Verify that you are properly grounded.

13. Unplug the power cord from the system unit.

14. Remove the top to the case.

15. Locate an available slot where you plan to install the network interface card.

16. Using the provided documentation, verify that the network interface card is configured to use the predetermined I/O address and an available IRQ.

17. Gently install the network interface card into the slot. Warning: Don't bend the card from side to side; only move the card back and forth from end to end.

18. Screw the mounting screw into place.

19. Replace the top of the case.

20. Plug in the system unit.

21. Power on the lab workstation, and allow it to boot into Windows 95.

22. If the workstation fails to boot properly, power cycle the PC, and when prompted choose **Safe Mode**.

Observing the I/O conflict

1. Start your lab workstation, and allow it to boot into Windows 95.

2. Click the **Start** button.

3. Point to **Settings**.

4. Click **Control Panel**.

5. Double-click the **System** icon.

6. Click the **Device Manager** tab.

7. Double-click the icon of the installed network card.

8. Click the **Resources** tab.

9. Observe the conflicting device list.

10. Click the **Cancel** button.

11. Close Device Manager and shut down Windows.

Resolving the I/O conflict

Your instructor will provide you with an available I/O address.

1. Unplug the power cord from the system unit.

2. Remove the top to the case.

3. Locate the network interface card.

4. Using the provided documentation configure the network interface card to use the I/O address specified by your instructor.

5. Replace the top of the case.

6. Plug in the system unit.

7. Power on the lab workstation, and allow it to boot into Windows 95.

8. If the workstation fails to boot properly, power cycle the PC, and when prompted choose **Safe Mode**.

Lab Notes

What is a power cycle? – The term power cycle refers to turning off and on the power to your PC.

What is an I/O address? – An I/O address is a memory address stored in RAM assigned to the operations of a particular device.

CERTIFICATION OBJECTIVES

Table 2-4   Core A+ objectives

Objective	Chapters	Page Numbers
1.3 Identify available IRQs, DMA's, and I/O addresses and procedures for configuring them for device installation, including identifying switch and jumper settings. Content may include the following:		
Standard IRQ settings	3	123
Locating and setting switches/jumpers	2, 6, 8	52, 63, 263, 388, 403, 409
Network Cards	1	8-9
1.8 Recognize the functions and effective use of common hand tools. Content may include the following:		
Torx bit	7	337
Regular bit	7	337
2.2 Identify basic troubleshooting procedures and good practices for eliciting problem symptoms from customers. Content may include the following:		
Troubleshooting/isolation/problem determination procedures	7	345
Determine whether hardware or software problem	7	349

REVIEW QUESTIONS

Circle True or False.

1. Only two devices at a time can use an I/O address. True / False

2. I/O stand for input/output. True / False

3. An I/O address is a physical location on the hard drive where the CPU will store data. True / False

4. Most all hardware devices need at least six I/O addresses to function properly. True / False

5. Describe the steps you would take to determine which hardware device or devices are conflicting with a particular component.

   _____

   _____

   _____

   _____

   _____

6. You have recently installed a new network interface card. You believe that its I/O address is conflicting with your sound card. Describe two ways you could quickly resolve this conflict without removing either component.

   _____

   _____

   _____

   _____

   _____

LAB 2.4 THE BOOT PROCESS

Objective

The objective of this lab exercise is to familiarize you with the boot process of a PC and to provide hands-on troubleshooting experience. After completing this lab exercise, you will be able to:

- Describe, in order, the PC boot process.

- Describe the effect that various defective components have on the boot process.

- Troubleshoot the PC boot process.

Materials Required

One Windows 95 lab workstation for every four students. The lab workstations should meet the following requirements:

- 486 or better
- At least 8MB of RAM
- 540MB or larger hard drive

One ESD mat for each lab workstation

Grounding straps for each student

Necessary tools for removing the lab workstation's case

Lab Setup & Safety Tips

- Each lab workstation should have Window 95 installed and functioning properly.

ACTIVITY

Observing the boot process

1. Turn on your PC.

2. Note the various startup screens.

3. Shut down your PC.

4. Verify that you are properly grounded.

5. Unplug the power cord from the system unit.

6. Remove the case.

7. Remove all of the SIMMS from your PC.

8. Restart your PC.

9. Record the effect of missing SIMMS:

_____

10. Shut down your PC.

11. Reinstall the SIMMs that you removed in step 7.

12. Restart your PC.

13. Note the effect of the replaced SIMMS.

14. Shut down your PC.

15. Reverse the hard drive cable at the systemboard.

16. Restart your PC.

17. Record the effect of the incorrect hard drive cabling:

_____

18. Shut down your PC.

19. Correctly install the hard drive cable at the systemboard.

20. Remove the hard drive cable from the hard drive.

21. Restart your PC.

22. Record the effect of the uninstalled hard drive cable:

_____

23. Shut down your PC.

24. Reinstall the hard drive cable at the hard drive.

25. Restart your PC.

26. Note the effect of the installed hard drive cable.

27. Remove the floppy drive cable from the systemboard.

28. Restart your PC.

29. Record the effect of the uninstalled floppy drive cable:

_____

30. Shut down your PC.

31. Reinstall the floppy drive cable.

32. Restart your PC.

33. Note the effect of the installed floppy drive cable.

34. Shut down your PC.

35. Remove the keyboard from the PC.

36. Restart your PC.

37. Record the effect of the uninstalled keyboard:

_____

38. Shut down your PC.

39. Reinstall the keyboard.

40. Restart your PC.

41. Note the effect of the installed keyboard.

Lab Notes

What is POST? – POST stands for power-on self-test. The POST is a self-diagnostic program used to perform a simple test of the CPU, RAM and various I/O devices. The POST is performed when the computer is first powered on.

CERTIFICATION OBJECTIVES

A+

Table 2-5   Core A+ objectives

Objective	Chapters	Page Numbers
1.1 Identify basic terms, concepts, and functions of system modules, including how each module should work during normal operation. Examples of concepts and modules:		
Memory	1, 3, 9	6-7, 105-107, 430-437, 439-441
1.2 Identify basic procedures for adding and removing field replaceable modules. Examples of modules:		
Memory	9, 14	473, 722
2.1 Identify common symptoms and problems associated with each module and how to troubleshoot and isolate the problems. Content may include the following:		
Processor/Memory symptoms	App. E	E14
Keyboards/Mouse/Track	App. E , 4, 7	E4, 5, 181, 351
Floppy drive failures	App. E, 4	E2, 161-165
Hard Drives	App. E , 6	E4, 313, 324
POST audible/visual error codes	App. A	A1
4.4 Identify the purpose of CMOS (Complementary Metal-Oxide Semiconductor), what it contains and how to change its basic parameters. Example Basic CMOS Settings:		
boot sequence	1, 3	7, 120-121

REVIEW QUESTIONS

Circle True or False.

1. A PC can function properly without any memory installed. True / False

2. Hard drive data cables are reversible. True / False

3. Floppy drive data cables are not reversible. True / False

4. If a PC is started without a keyboard attached, you will receive an error message during the POST. True / False

5. What one component from the previous activity will completely halt all system activities?

_____

_____

_____

_____

6. You just finished moving a PC from one building to another. You have not changed any of the PC's hardware configurations, but now when you start the system it gives you a keyboard/mouse error. If the keyboard and mouse are plugged in, what could be the problem?

_____

_____

_____

_____

THE SYSTEMBOARD

LABS INCLUDED IN THIS CHAPTER

LAB 3.1 COMPONENT IDENTIFICATION

LAB 3.2 CPU IDENTIFICATION AND INSTALLATION

LAB 3.3 BUS IDENTIFICATION AND PCI EXPANSION CARD INSTALLATION

LAB 3.1   COMPONENT IDENTIFICATION

Objective

The objective of this lab exercise is to provide you with the ability to identify various components of the systemboard from several different generations of personal computers. After completing this lab exercise, you will be able to:

- Identify the major components of systemboards from different generations.

Materials Required

One Windows 95 lab workstation for every four students. The lab workstations should meet the following requirements:

- 486 or better
- At least 8MB of RAM
- 540MB or larger hard drive

Systemboard documentation for each of the lab workstations. You will need to be able to identify the location and purpose of each jumper block on the systemboard.

Each group of students will require a packet of labels.

Any available systemboards from each of the following generations:

- PC
- PC-AT
- 286
- 386
- 486
- Pentium
- Pentium II

Lab Setup and Safety Tips

- To create the instructor's display, arrange the available systemboards with the following components labeled:

  - ISA expansion bus
  - PCI expansion bus
  - VLB expansion bus
  - Bus control chip set
  - System BIOS
  - Keyboard BIOS
  - Battery
  - DRAM
  - SIMMS
  - DIMMS
  - Keyboard connector
  - Mouse connector
  - Cache memory
  - Integrated IDE controller
  - Integrated floppy drive controller
  - Integrated I/O connectors
  - Power supply
  - RAM slots
  - CPU socket

ACTIVITY

Viewing the instructor's display

1. Record at least one hardware difference between each of the systemboard generations.

PC _____

_____

_____

PC-AT _____

_____

_____

286 _____

_____

_____

386 _____

_____

_____

486 _____

_____

_____

Pentium _____

_____

_____

Pentium II _____

_____

_____

Labeling the lab workstation

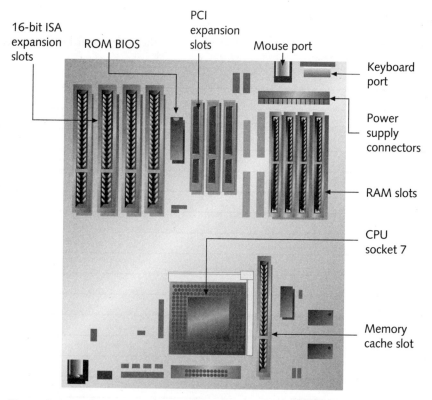

Figure 3-1 A Pentium systemboard with no components added

Labeling your workstation components

1. Label each of your lab workstation's components as shown above.

Labeling the jumper blocks

1. Refer to the provided documentation and label each of your lab workstation's jumper blocks.

Lab Notes

Table 3-1 Major manufacturers of systemboards

Manufacturer	Product	Web Address
Acer America Corp.	Pentium boards	www.acer.com
American Megatrends	486, Pentium boards	www.megatrends.com
ASUS	486, Pentium boards	www.asus.com
First International Computer, Inc.	486, Pentium boards	www.fica.com
Giga-Byte Technology, Co.	Pentium boards	www.giga-byte.com
Intel Corporation	Pentium boards	www.intel.com
Micronics Computers	Pentium boards	www.micronics.com
Ocean Office Automation, Ltd.	486, Pentium boards	www.ocean-usa.com
Supermicro Computers, Inc.	Pentium boards	www.supermicro.com
Tyan Computer	Pentium boards	www.tyan.com

Table 3-2   The Intel chip set family

Common Name	Model Number	Comments
Triton I	430FX	The oldest chip set, no longer produced
Triton II	430HX	High performance, supports dual CPUs
Triton III	430VX	Value chip set, supports SDRAM
	430MX	Used for notebooks (M=mobile)
	430TX	Supports SDRAM, ultra DMA; replaces the VX and MX
Natoma	440FX	Supports Pentium Pro and Pentium II
Orion	450GX, KX	Supports Pentium Pro

CERTIFICATION OBJECTIVES

Table 3-3   Core A+ objectives

Objective	Chapters	Page Numbers
1.1 Identify basic terms, concepts, and functions of system modules, including how each module should work during normal operation. Examples of concepts and modules:		
Systemboard	1, 3	4-8, 38, 84-124
Power supply	1, 3	10, 37, 124
Processor/CPU	1, 3	6, 37, 87-96
Memory	1, 3, 9	6-7, 105-107, 430-437, 439-441
Storage devices	1, 4, 5	10-11, 142, 191-249
Monitor	1, 4	2, 175
Modem	1, 15	8, 763
Input devices	1, 4	2, 172, 179
Output devices	1	2
BIOS	1, 2, 3	6, 56, 61, 99-105
1.2 Identify basic procedures for adding and removing field replaceable modules. Examples of modules:		
Systemboard	14	728
Power supply	10	498-500
Processor /CPU	14	719
Memory	9, 14	473, 722
Storage devices	6, 14	261-267, 733-739
Monitor	14	748

Table 3-3   Core A+ objectives (continued)

Objective	Chapters	Page Numbers
4.3 Identify the most popular type of motherboards, their components, and their architecture (e.g., bus structures and power supplies). Content may include the following: Components:		
Communication ports	3, 14	119, 732
Processor Sockets	3	95
External Cache Memory		
(Level 2)	3	107
ROM	3	103
ISA	3	109-111, 115, 116
EISA	3	112, 116
PCI	3	114-116
VESA local bus (VL-BUS)	3	112, 116

REVIEW QUESTIONS

Circle True or False.

1. The mouse and keyboard ports are always located immediately next to the CPU socket. True / False

2. Systemboards require two power connectors from the power supply. True / False

3. Different systemboards can use different types of memory. True / False

4. ISA slots are shorter in length than PCI slots. True / False

5. Most CPUs are bolted to the systemboard to eliminate a chance of it slipping off and causing the entire PC to crash. True / False

6. You are employed at Cold Sweet Ice Company as a helpdesk technician. Jamie, one of your favorite customers wants to install more memory into her PC but doesn't know how to attach it to the systemboard. Describe below the steps Jamie will need to follow in order to locate the memory slots.

_____

_____

_____

_____

_____

LAB 3.2   CPU IDENTIFICATION AND INSTALLATION

Objective

The objective of this lab exercise is to provide you with the ability to identify the various central processing units (CPUs), or microprocessors, and their corresponding mounting technologies from the different generations of personal computers. After completing this lab exercise, you will be able to:

- Identify the various generations of CPUs, or microprocessors, used in PCs.
- Identify the various generations of CPU mounting technology used in PCs.
- Install and remove a 486 CPU.

Materials Required

One Windows 95 lab workstation for every four students. The lab workstations should meet the following requirements:

- 486 or better
- At least 8MB of RAM
- 540MB or larger hard drive

One grounding strap for each student

One chip pulling tool for each lab workstation

One grounding mat for each lab workstation

Any available CPUs from each of the following families:

- 8088
- 80286
- 80386
- 80486
- Pentium
- Pentium Pro
- Pentium II

Lab Setup and Safety Tips

- Each lab workstation should have Window 95 installed and functioning properly.
- Arrange the CPUs and the matching mounting technology, labeling each so that students can inspect them.
- Always unplug the power cord before touching components within the case.

ACTIVITY

Viewing the instructor's display

1. Inspect each of the available CPUs, noting their characteristics.
2. Also note the mounting technology associated with the respective CPUs, and the mounting technology characteristics.

Removing your workstation's CPU

1. Power off your lab workstation.
2. Unplug the power cord from the system unit.
3. Verify that you are properly grounded.

4. Remove the case from your lab workstation.

5. Locate the CPU.

6. Release the heat sink from the top of the CPU (if the heat sink doesn't come off with ease, leave it on top of the CPU).

7. Release the ZIF lever.

8. Note how the CPU is currently installed. This will be important when you are trying to reinstall the CPU. Specifically note the direction that the writing on the CPU is facing.

9. Use the chip pulling tool to remove your CPU. Warning: When removing your CPU, pull evenly straight up on the CPU; do not bend from side to side.

10. Stand clear of the case and plug in the power cord.

11. Power on the PC and observe the results of a PC without a CPU.

Reinstalling your workstation's CPU

1. Remembering which direction the CPU should be facing, gently slide it back into position.

2. Don't force the CPU. If it is not moving into place with ease, check for bent pins on the bottom of the CPU.

3. Lock the CPU into position using the ZIF lever.

4. Replace the heat sink on top of the CPU, if necessary.

5. Test the installation before replacing the case.

6. Stand clear of the case and plug in the power cord

7. Power on the PC and verify that the system boots properly.

8. Power off the PC and remove the power cord.

9. Replace the case.

10. Plug in the system unit.

11. Power on the system unit.

12. Power off the PC.

Lab Notes

Table 3-4   The Intel Pentium family of chips

Processor	Current Clock Speeds	MMX	Primary Cache
Classic Pentium	100, 120, 133, 150, 166, 200	No	16K
Pentium MMX	150, 166, 200	Yes	32K
Pentium Pro	166, 180, 200	No	16K
Pentium II	166, 180, 200, 266, 300	Yes	32K
Deschutes	Expecting 300, 333, 400	Yes	Unknown

How do I control the CPU settings? – Most CPU's are configured using jumper blocks or DIP switches located directly on the systemboard.

Do I always need a heat sink? – Any CPU, starting with a 486 and moving up, requires a heat sink to maintain the proper CPU temperature.

What is the correct voltage for my CPU? – CPU voltage varies depending on the brand name and generation of the CPU. Consult the documentation for your CPU.

CERTIFICATION OBJECTIVES

Table 3-5   Core A+ objectives

Objective	Chapters	Page Numbers
1.1 Identify basic terms, concepts, and functions of system modules, including how each module should work during normal operation. Examples of concepts and modules:		
Systemboard	1, 3	4-8, 38, 84-124
Processor/CPU	1, 3	6, 37, 87-96
1.2 Identify basic procedures for adding and removing field replaceable modules. Examples of modules:		
Processor/CPU	14	719
1.3 Identify available IRQs, DMAs, and I/O addresses and procedures for configuring them for device installation, including identifying switch and jumper settings. Content may include the following:		
Locating and setting switches/jumpers	2, 6, 8	52, 63, 263, 388, 403, 409
1.8 Recognize the functions and effective use of common hand tools. Content may include the following:		
Chip puller	7	337
Torx bit	7	337
Regular bit	7	337
4.1 Distinguish between the popular CPU chips in terms of their basic characteristics. Content may include the following:		
Popular CPU chips:		
386	3	88, 89
486	3	88, 89
586	3	88, 90-91
686	3	92
Characteristics:		
Physical size	3	95
Voltage	3, 14	96, 717
Speeds	3	89-93
Heat sink and cooling fan requirements	3	94
On board cache or not	3, 14	90, 92, 93, 717
Sockets	3	95
Number of pins	3	95

REVIEW QUESTIONS

Circle True or False.

1. All CPUs are the same size. True / False

2. CPU voltage varies depending on the generation and brand name. True / False

3. Chip pullers are used to remove the heat sink for the top of the CPU. True / False

4. ZIF sockets are used to connect the memory to the systemboard. True / False

5. Which is faster: the 8088 processor or the 486 processor?

   _____

   _____

   _____

   _____

   _____

6. You are currently employed as a PC support technician at the Heavenly Palace Factory. Your supervisor wants to upgrade his 486 computer to a Pentium 166. He has asked you to tell him the parts that he will need to purchase for this upgrade. List below the minimum parts your supervisor will need to purchase in order to complete this upgrade.

   _____

   _____

   _____

   _____

   _____

7. You are at your local computer store and are considering upgrading your home PC to a Pentium Pro. Will you be able to use the CPU cooling fan from your 486 at home on the Pentium Pro chip?

   _____

   _____

   _____

   _____

LAB 3.3 BUS IDENTIFICATION AND PCI EXPANSION CARD INSTALLATION

Objective

The objective of this lab exercise is to allow you a hands-on opportunity to view and identify the different types of PC expansion buses. After completing this lab exercise, you will be able to:

- Identify the various expansion buses used in PCs.
- Describe the various components of the respective expansion buses.
- Install a PCI expansion card.

Materials Required

One Windows 95 lab workstation for every four students. The lab workstations should meet the following requirements:

- 486 or better
- At least 8MB of RAM
- 540MB or larger hard drive

One PCI expansion card of any kind

One ESD mat for every lab workstation

One grounding strap for each student

Any available systemboards from each of the following generations:

(Note: These systemboards will be used for an activity.)

- PC
- PC-AT
- IBM PC
- 286
- 386
- 486
- Pentium
- Pentium II

Lab Setup & Safety Tips

- Each lab workstation should have Windows 95 installed and functioning properly.
- Arrange the systemboards with their respective expansion buses and corresponding control chip sets so students can inspect them.
- Students must comply with standard ESD procedures.
- Always unplug the power cord before touching components within the case.

ACTIVITY

Getting to know expansion buses

1. Inspect and note the characteristics of the following architectures:

   - ISA 8-bit expansion bus
   - ISA 16-bit expansion bus
   - VLB expansion bus and its control chip set

- PCI expansion bus and its control chip set
- MCA expansion bus and its control chip set

2. After the labels on the display are removed and then rearranged, match the labels to their corresponding expansion buses.

Installing a PCI expansion card

1. Power off your PC.

2. Verify that you are properly grounded.

3. Unplug the power cord from the system unit.

4. Remove the top to the case.

5. Locate an available PCI slot where you plan to install the PCI expansion card.

6. Gently install the PCI expansion card into the slot. Warning: Don't bend the card from side to side; only move the card back and forth or from end to end.

7. Screw the mounting screw into place.

8. Replace the top of the case.

9. Plug in the system unit.

10. Power on the lab workstation and allow it to boot into Windows 95.

Removing the PCI expansion card

1. Power off your PC.

2. Verify that you are properly grounded.

3. Unplug the power cord from the system unit.

4. Remove the top to the case.

5. Unscrew the mounting screw from the frame.

6. Gently remove the PCI expansion card from the PCI slot. Warning: Don't bend the card from side to side; only move the card back and forth or from end to end.

7. Replace the top of the case.

8. Plug in the system unit.

9. Power on the lab workstation, and allow it to boot into Windows 95.

Lab Notes

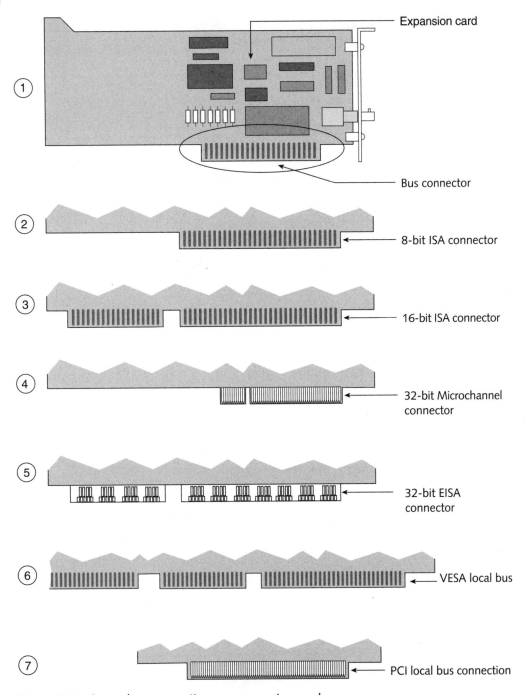

Figure 3-2   Seven bus connections on expansion cards

CERTIFICATION OBJECTIVES

Table 3-6   Core A+ objectives

Objective	Chapters	Page Numbers
4.3 Identify the most popular type of motherboards, their components, and their architecture (e.g., bus structures and power supplies). Content may include the following: Components:		
Communication ports	3, 14	119, 732
Bus Architecture	3	108-117
ISA	3	109-111, 115, 116
EISA	3	112, 116
PCI	3	114-116
VESA local bus (VL-BUS)	3	112, 116
Basic compatibility guidelines	3	102

REVIEW QUESTIONS

Circle True or False.

1. ISA is always faster than PCI. True / False

2. Microchannel is a 64-bit bus. True / False

3. Microchannel and EISA can use the same expansion slot. True / False

4. An ISA expansion card can be either 8-bit or 16-bit. True / False

5. John wants to add a sound card to his 386. Before purchasing the sound card, he is going to look at his systemboard to find out what type he should purchase. Describe to John how to tell if he has an 8-bit or a 16-bit ISA expansion slot on his systemboard.

_____

_____

_____

_____

_____

6. What is one advantage of using PCI over ISA?

_____

_____

_____

_____

_____

CHAPTER FOUR

FLOPPY DRIVES AND OTHER ESSENTIAL DEVICES

LABS INCLUDED IN THIS CHAPTER

LAB 4.1 CONFIGURING A SINGLE FLOPPY DRIVE

LAB 4.2 CONFIGURING A DUAL FLOPPY DRIVE SYSTEM

LAB 4.1   CONFIGURING A SINGLE FLOPPY DRIVE

Objective

The objective of this lab is to provide you with the hands-on experience of removing, installing and configuring a floppy drive. After completing this lab exercise, you will be able to:

- Install a single floppy disk drive in a PC.

- Configure a single floppy drive to function properly within a PC system.

- Remove a single floppy disk drive from a PC.

Materials Required

One Windows 95 lab workstation for every four students. The lab workstations should meet the following requirements:

- 486 or better
- At least 8MB of RAM
- 540MB or larger hard drive

Necessary data cable and controller to allow for a 5.25 floppy drive installation

One ESD mat for each lab workstation

One grounding strap for each student

One 5.25 inch, 1.2 MB floppy disk drive for each lab workstation

One 5.25 floppy disk

Necessary tool to remove the case and mount/dismount of floppy drives

Lab Setup & Safety Tips

- Each lab workstation should have Window 95 installed and be functioning properly.

- Each lab workstation should have one 3.5 floppy drive installed and functioning properly.

- Each lab workstation should have one available 5.25 bay.

- Each group of students should be given one 5.25 floppy drive.

- Students must comply with standard ESD procedures.

- Always unplug the power cord before touching components within the case.

ACTIVITY

Removing the 3.5 floppy drive

1. Power off your PC.

2. Verify that you are properly grounded.

3. Unplug the power cord from the system unit.

4. Remove the top of the case.

5. Unplug the data cable connected to the 3.5 floppy drive.

6. Unplug the power connector for the 3.5 floppy drive.

7. Dismount the 3.5 floppy drive.

8. Remove the 3.5 floppy drive from your lab workstation.

9. Stand clear of the case and plug in the power cord.

10. Power on your lab workstation, and enter the CMOS setup program.

11. Remove the 3.5 floppy drive from the setup program.

12. Save your changes and reboot your lab workstation.

Removing the 3.5 floppy drive from Windows

1. Allow your lab workstation to boot into Windows 95.

2. Double-click the **My Computer** icon.

3. Verify that Windows 95 does not recognize any floppy drives.

4. If there is still an icon for the 3.5 floppy drive, do the following steps:

   a. Click the **Start** button.

   b. Point to **Settings** and click **Control Panel.**

   c. Double-click the **System** icon.

   d. Click the **Device Manager** tab.

   e. Double-click the **Floppy disk controller** icon.

   f. Click the 3.5 floppy drive icon to highlight it.

   g. Press **Delete**.

   h. Click the **Yes** button on the confirmation message.

   i. Reboot your lab workstation, then double-click the **My Computer** icon to verify that Windows doesn't recognize any floppy drives.

Installing a 5.25 floppy drive

1. Power off your PC.

2. Verify that you are properly grounded.

3. Unplug the power cord from the system unit.

4. Remove the top of the case.

5. Locate an available 5.25 drive bay.

6. Remove any blanks that may be in place.

7. Slide the 5.25 floppy drive into the bay.

8. Plug in the data cable.

9. Plug in the power connector.

10. Stand clear of the case and plug in the power cord.

11. Power on your lab workstation.

12. Enter the CMOS setup program.

13. Configure the setup program to recognize the 5.25 floppy drive.

14. Save the CMOS settings and reboot your lab workstation.

Testing the 5.25 floppy drive

1. Allow your lab workstation to boot into Windows 95.

2. Double-click the **My Computer** icon.

3. Verify that Windows 95 recognizes the 5.25 floppy drive.

4. Insert the 5.25 floppy disk into the 5.25 floppy drive.

5. Right-click the 5.25 floppy drive icon, and select **Format**.

6. Click the **Start** button in the Format dialog box.

7. When the formatting is complete, click the **Close** button.

8. In the Format dialog box, click the **Close** button.

9. Close the My Computer window.

If Windows 95 does not detect the floppy drive

1. Click the **Start** button.

2. Point to **Settings** and click **Control Panel**.

3. Double-click the **Add New Hardware** icon.

4. Click the **Next** button three times to allow Windows to detect new hardware.

5. When the process is complete, allow Windows to install the proper device driver.

6. Reboot your lab workstation, and follow the steps in the section, "Testing the 5.25 floppy drive."

Lab Notes

How do I know which way to connect a data cable? – All PC data cables have a red stripe along one side of the cable. This stripe should always be aligned with the number one pin on the attached device.

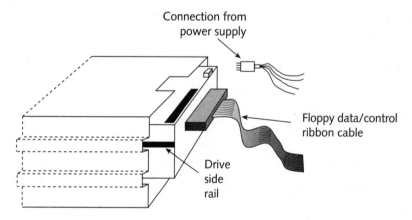

Figure 4-1   Floppy drive, data cable, and power connection

CERTIFICATION OBJECTIVES

Table 4-1   Core A+ objectives

Objective	Chapters	Page Numbers
4.4 Identify the purpose of CMOS (Complementary Metal-Oxide Semiconductor), what it contains and how to change its basic parameters. Example Basic CMOS Settings:		
floppy drive – enable/disable drive or boot, speed, density	1, 3	7, 120-121
boot sequence	1, 3	7, 120-121

Table 4-2 DOS/Windows A+ objectives

Objective	Chapters	Page Numbers
3.3 Identify the basic system boot sequences for DOS, Windows 3.x, and Windows 95, and alternative ways to boot the system software. Content may include the following:		
Booting a system from floppy or hard drive	2	66, 70
3.4 Identify how Windows 95 uses plug and play, and how it functions. Content may include the following:		
BIOS/OS recognizes peripherals and loads appropriate drivers and assigns system resources	11	562, 563
When working properly	11	563
When not working properly	11	564, 568

REVIEW QUESTIONS

Circle True or False.

1. When you install a floppy drive, you must enter the CMOS setup program. True / False

2. All floppy drives need three cables: two data cables and one power connector. True / False

3. The boot sequence can be effected when a floppy drive is added or remove from a PC. True / False

4. You can use the Add New Hardware icon on Control Panel to allow Windows to automatically detect new hardware. True / False

5. What must you do after physically installing a floppy drive?

   _____

   _____

   _____

   _____

   _____

6. Stacey just installed a floppy drive into her PC, but the floppy drive icon does not show up when she boots into Windows. Assuming that she installed the drive correctly, what would you recommend Stacey do to make Windows recognize her new floppy drive?

   _____

   _____

   _____

   _____

   _____

LAB 4.2   CONFIGURING A DUAL FLOPPY DRIVE SYSTEM

Objective

The objective of this lab is to provide you with the hands-on skills necessary to configure dual floppy drives on a personal computer. After completing this lab exercise you will be able to:

- Install dual floppy disk drives in a personal computer.
- Properly configure a personal computer to use two floppy disk drives.

Materials Required

One Windows 95 lab workstation for every four students. The lab workstations should meet the following requirements:

- 486 or better
- At least 8MB of RAM
- 540MB or larger hard drive

Necessary data cables and controllers to allow for a 5.25 and a 3.5 floppy drive installation

One ESD mat for each lab workstation

One grounding strap for each student

One 3.5 inch, 1.44 MB floppy disk drive for each lab workstation

One 5.25 floppy disk

One 3.5 floppy disk

Necessary tool to remove the case and mount/dismount floppy drives

Lab Setup & Safety Tips

- Each lab workstation should have Window 95 installed and functioning properly.
- Each lab workstation should have one 5.25 floppy drive installed and functioning properly.
- Each lab workstation should have one available 3.5 bay.
- Each group of students should be given one 3.5 floppy drive.
- Students must comply with standard ESD procedures.
- Always unplug the power cord before touching components within the case.

ACTIVITY

Installing a 3.5 floppy drive

1. Power off your PC.
2. Verify that you are properly grounded.
3. Unplug the power cord from the system unit.
4. Remove the top of the case.
5. Locate an available 3.5 drive bay.
6. Remove any blanks that may be in place.
7. Slide the 3.5 floppy drive into the bay.
8. Plug in the data cable.

9. Plug in the power connector.

10. Stand clear of the case and plug in the power cord.

11. Power on your lab workstation.

12. Enter the CMOS setup program.

13. Configure the setup program to recognize the 3.5 floppy drive.

14. Save the CMOS settings and reboot your lab workstation.

Testing the 3.5 floppy drive

1. Allow your lab workstation to boot into Windows 95.

2. Double-click the **My Computer** icon.

3. Verify that Windows 95 recognizes the 3.5 floppy drive.

4. Insert the 3.5 floppy disk into the 3.5 floppy drive.

5. Right-click the 3.5 floppy drive icon and select **Format**.

6. Click the **Start** button in the Format dialog box.

7. When the formatting is complete, click the **Close** button.

8. In the Format dialog box, click the **Close** button.

9. Close the My Computer window.

Testing the 5.25 floppy drive as drive B

1. Allow your lab workstation to boot into Windows 95.

2. Double-click the **My Computer** icon.

3. Verify that Windows 95 recognizes the 5.25 floppy drive.

4. Insert the 5.25 floppy disk into the 5.25 floppy drive.

5. Right-click the 5.25 floppy drive icon, and select **Format**.

6. Click the **Start** button in the Format dialog box.

7. When the formatting is complete, click the **Close** button.

8. In the Format dialog box, click the **Close** button.

9. Close the My Computer window.

If Windows 95 does not detect the floppy drive

1. Click the **Start** button.

2. Point to **Settings** and click **Control Panel**.

3. Double-click the **Add New Hardware** icon.

4. Click the **Next** button three times to allow Windows to detect the new hardware.

5. When the process is complete, allow Windows to install the proper device driver.

6. Reboot your lab workstation, and follow the steps in the section, "Testing the 3.5 floppy drive."

Lab Notes

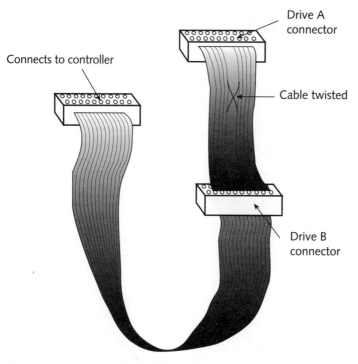

Figure 4-2 Twist in the cable

How do I configure two floppy drives using the same data cable? – The figure above shows an example of a typical floppy drive cable that could be used to configure multiple drives with the same data cable. Note that the twist in the data cable helps the computer differentiate between floppy drive A and B.

CERTIFICATION OBJECTIVES

Table 4-3 Core A+ objectives

Objective	Chapters	Page Numbers
4.4 Identify the purpose of CMOS (Complementary Metal-Oxide Semiconductor), what it contains and how to change its basic parameters. Example Basic CMOS Settings:		
Floppy drive – enable/disable drive or boot, speed, density	1, 3	7, 120-121
Boot sequence	1, 3	7, 120-121

Table 4-4   DOS/Windows A+ objectives

Objective	Chapters	Page Numbers
3.3 Identify the basic system boot sequences for DOS, Windows 3.x, and Windows 95, and alternative ways to boot the system software. Content may include the following:		
Booting a system from floppy, hard drive	2	66, 70
3.4 Identify how Windows 95 uses plug and play, and how it functions. Content may include the following:		
BIOS/OS recognizes peripherals and loads appropriate drivers and assigns system resources	11	562, 563
When working properly	11	563
When not working properly	11	564, 568

REVIEW QUESTIONS

Circle True or False.

1. PCs always boot to drive B first. True / False

2. Your drive A is always a hard drive. True / False

3. A PC can only have two floppy drives. True / False

4. A 3.5 floppy disk holds more data than a 5.25 floppy disk. True / False

5. Alice, who uses Windows 95, wants to know how to format a 3.5-inch floppy disk. List the steps below.

_____

_____

_____

_____

_____

6. Dave has recently removed one of his floppy drives from his PC. He now receives an error message every time he reboots his computer. What would you recommend Dave does in order to eliminate this error message?

_____

_____

_____

_____

_____

INTRODUCTION TO HARD DRIVES

LABS INCLUDED IN THIS CHAPTER

LAB 5.1 HARD DRIVE MANAGEMENT

LAB 5.2 HARD DRIVE PREPARATION AND OPTIMIZATION

LAB 5.3 HARD DRIVE ORGANIZATION

LAB 5.4 REMOVABLE DRIVE CONFIGURATION

LAB 5.1 HARD DRIVE MANAGEMENT

Objective

The FDISK utility allows you to add, remove and view your hard drive's partition configuration. After completing this lab exercise, you will be able to:

- Use the FDISK utility to view drive configuration information.
- Add and remove partitions using the FDISK utility.
- Use the FDISK utility to set a partition active.
- Describe the relationship between a logical drive and an extended partition.

Materials Required

This lab exercise requires one complete lab workstation for every four students. The lab workstation should meet the following requirements:

- 486 or better
- 8MB of RAM
- Windows 95

The DOS system disk created in Lab 1.2

Lab Setup & Safety Tips

- Each workstation's hard drive should contain at least one partition.
- Warning: The steps in the following Activity will erase all data currently stored on your lab workstation. Back up data before proceeding.
- Any changes made using the FDISK utility will effect the data stored on the partition or partitions that were modified. BE CAREFUL!

ACTIVITY

Viewing the current hard drive configuration

1. Power off your lab workstation.
2. Insert the boot disk into drive A.
3. Power on your lab workstation and allow it to boot from the floppy disk.
4. At the A prompt, type **FDISK**.
5. From the FDISK menu, select option 4 by typing the number **4** and pressing **Enter**.
6. Observe your current hard drive configuration.

Deleting a partition

1. Press the **Esc** key to return to the main menu.
2. From the FDISK main menu, select option 3 by typing the number **3** and pressing **Enter**.

3. Select the primary partition on your hard drive by typing in number **1** and pressing **Enter**.

4. Type the volume label of the primary partition.

5. Confirm deletion by typing the letter "**Y**" and pressing **Enter**.

6. Press the **Esc** key to return to the main menu.

7. Press **Esc** again to exit the FDISK utility. The workstation will then be restarted.

8. Press the spacebar to restart the computer.

Creating a partition

1. Boot the workstation using the floppy disk again.

2. At the A prompt, type **FDISK**.

3. At the FDISK main menu, select option **1** and press **Enter**.

4. When the FDISK utility asks if you would like to use all of the available space for the primary partition and set it active, select No by typing **N** and pressing **Enter**.

5. When FDISK prompts you to enter the amount of drive space you would like to use, type **500** and press **Enter**.

6. When prompted for a volume label, type **DRIVE 1** and press **Enter**.

7. Press **Esc** to return to the FDISK main menu.

Setting an active partition

1. Select option **2** from the FDISK main menu.

2. Choose the primary partition that you created by typing number **1** and pressing **Enter**.

3. Press **Esc** to exit FDISK and your workstation will be restarted.

Lab Notes

Extended partition – An extended partition is a section of the hard drive that allows the partitioning of logical drives. Note that there can be only one extended partition per hard drive.

Logical drive – A logical drive is a partition that holds a drive letter and behaves as a separate physical drive. Note that logical drives can only be created within extended partitions.

Active partition – If a partition is set active, the system will attempt to boot from that partition.

FDISK /MBR – This command is used to refresh the master boot record without causing any data loss.

CERTIFICATION OBJECTIVES

Table 5-1   Dos/Windows A+ objectives

Objective	Chapters	Page Numbers
1.5 Identify the procedures for basic disk management. Content may include the following:		
Using disk management utilities	5, 6	220, 277-289
Partitioning	6	268
3.1 Identify the procedures for installing DOS, Windows 3.x, and Windows 95, and bringing the software to a basic operational level. Content may include the following:		
Partition	5	220, 268-271
4.6 Identify the purpose of and procedures for using various DOS and Windows-based utilities and commands/switches to diagnose and troubleshoot problems. Content may include the following:		
DOS:		
Fdisk.exe	4, 5, 6	161, 195, 233, 168-270, 318, 319

REVIEW QUESTIONS

Circle True or False.

1. When a partition's size is changed using the FDISK utility, the data contained on the partition is lost. True / False

2. The FDISK utility is used to partition and format hard drives. True / False

3. The FDISK utility refers to hard drive capacity in bytes. True / False

4. Extended partitions are always placed with logical drives. True / False

5. List three functions of the FDISK utility.

   _____

   _____

   _____

   _____

   _____

6. What will happen if an active partition is not set?

   _____

   _____

   _____

   _____

   _____

7. You are the desktop PC support technician for the Good Job Corporation. John, one of your customers, suspects that his hard drive is not partitioned to use its full capacity. Describe how you would use the FDISK utility to show your customer his current hard drive configuration.

_____

_____

_____

_____

_____

8. Describe the relationship between a logical drive and an extended partition.

_____

_____

_____

_____

_____

5

LAB 5.2   HARD DRIVE PREPARATION AND OPTIMIZATION

Objective

Formatting a hard drive is the procedure used to install a file system onto a newly partitioned hard drive. In this lab exercise you will learn how to properly install and optimize the FAT file system. After completing this lab exercise, you will be able to:

- Format a partition.
- Use and describe how the SCANDISK utility can be used to optimize drive performance.
- Use and describe how the DEFRAG utility can be used to optimize drive performance.

Materials Required

This lab exercise requires a minimum of one complete lab workstation for each student.

One DOS boot disk that includes the Format command.

One DOS disk that contains both the SCANDISK and DEFRAG utilities.

Lab Setup & Safety Tips

- Each workstation's hard drive should contain one unformatted primary partition that has been set active.
- Be sure that the data stored on your lab workstation has been backed up before proceeding with this lab exercise.

ACTIVITY

Formatting the C drive

1. Power off your lab workstation.
2. Insert the boot disk into drive A.
3. Power on your lab workstation and allow it to boot from your DOS boot disk.
4. At the A prompt, type **FORMAT C:**.
5. When asked to confirm before proceeding, type **Y** and press **Enter**. The format command will begin to format drive C.
6. When formatting is complete, type a volume label of **DRIVE 1**.

Making drive C bootable

There are many different commands that can be used to make a drive bootable. The following includes two examples:

Example 1

1. Power off your lab workstation.
2. Insert the boot disk into drive A.
3. Power on your lab workstation and allow it to boot from your DOS boot disk.
4. At the A prompt, type **SYS A: C:** and press **Enter**.

Example 2

The /S switch tells DOS to SYS the drive after it has been formatted. Use the /? option to view other FORMAT switches.

1. Power off your lab workstation.

2. Insert the boot disk into drive A.

3. Power on your lab workstation and allow it to boot from your DOS boot disk.

4. At the A prompt, type **FORMAT C: /S**.

5. When asked to confirm before proceeding type **Y** and press **Enter**.

6. When formatting is complete, type in a volume label of **DRIVE 1**.

Using the SCANDISK utility

1. Put in the disk that contains the SCANDISK utility.

2. At the A prompt, type **SCANDISK** and press **Enter**.

3. Allow SCANDISK to verify your file and directory structure.

4. When SCANDISK has completed, use the **view log** option to view any errors that SCANDISK might have encountered.

5. After viewing the view log, exit the SCANDISK utility.

Using the DEFRAG utility

1. Put in the disk that contains the DEFRAG utility.

2. At the A prompt, type **DEFRAG** and press **Enter**.

3. Allow DEFRAG to reorganize the hard drive (this should go quickly if the drive was just recently formatted).

4. When the defragmentation is complete, exit the DEFRAG utility.

Lab Notes

What is a switch? – A switch is a parameter or variable that can be added to the end of a DOS command that will change or enhance the meaning of the command.

DEFRAG – This utility is designed to optimize file access by moving file clusters into a continuous chain, thus speeding up data retrieval. This utility should be used at least once a month to maintain optimum performance.

SCANDISK – This utility is designed to search a hard drive for lost or cross-linked clusters and attempt to repair them. This utility should be used at least once a month to maintain optimum performance.

Note that the use of the SCANDISK and DEFRAG utilities can improve system performance.

Table 5-2   Dos/Windows A+ objectives

Objective	Chapters	Page Numbers
1.5 Identify the procedures for basic disk management. Content may include the following:		
Using disk management utilities	5, 6	220, 277-289
Defragmenting	5, 6, 7	220, 221, 312, 338, 527
Scandisk	4, 5, 6	153, 223, 310
3.1 Identify the procedures for installing DOS, Windows 3.x, and Windows 95, and bringing the software to a basic operational level. Content may include the following:		
Format drive	4, 5, 7	146, 151, 165, 220, 338
4.6 Identify the purpose of and procedures for using various DOS- and Windows-based utilities and commands/switches to diagnose and troubleshoot problems. Content may include the following: DOS:		
Scandisk	4, 5, 7	153, 161, 223-324, 338
Defrag.exe	5, 6, 7	221-222, 251, 290, 312, 338

REVIEW QUESTIONS

Circle True or False.

1. Using the SCANDISK utility will delete all files less than 512 K in size. True / False

2. The DEFRAG utility places file clusters in consecutive order. True / False

3. The SCANDISK utility should only be ran once every three months. True / False

4. Newly created partition always need to be formatted before an operating system can be installed. True / False

5. Describe the functionality of the DEFRAG utility.

_____

_____

_____

_____

_____

6. You are currently employed as a PC desktop support technician at the Our World Corporation. One of your customers, Jamie, calls to tell you that her computer is running slower than it used to last month. List two things that might help improve the performance of Jamie's computer.

_____

_____

_____

_____

_____

5

7. John is currently running DEFRAG, and it is taking a really long time. John calls you to ask what the DEFRAG program is doing and why it is taking so long. Note that over the last year John has never ran the DEFRAG utility. Describe to John the purpose of the DEFRAG utility and explain why it is taking so long.

_____

_____

_____

_____

_____

LAB 5.3 HARD DRIVE ORGANIZATION

Objective

The objective of this lab exercise is to provide you with the installation, configuration and navigation experience necessary to control the DOS environment. After completing this lab exercise, you will be able to:

- Navigate the DOS directory structure.
- Identify DOS system files.
- Explain DOS file naming conventions, and rename both files and directories.
- Manipulate file attributes in the DOS environment.

Materials Required

This lab exercise requires one lab workstation for every four students. The lab workstation should meet the following requirements:

- 486 or better
- 4MB of RAM
- One formatted 540MB or larger hard drive
- DOS 5.0 or higher

Lab Setup & Safety Tips

- Each lab workstation should have DOS 5.0, or later, installed and functioning properly.

ACTIVITY

Navigating through the DOS environment

1 MORE

1. To briefly observe the DOS directory structure, type **TREE C:** at the C prompt and press **Enter**. The result will be a diagram of the current directory structure of your hard drive.

2. Boot your lab workstation to the C prompt.

3. Create a directory called Student. Type **MD STUDENT** and press **Enter**.

4. Observe where the Student directory is now located in the DOS directory structure. Type **TREE c:** and press **Enter**.

5. Change to the Student directory. Type **CD STUDENT** and press **Enter**.

6. Copy the Config.sys file to the Student directory. Type **COPY C:\CONFIG.SYS C:\STUDENT** and press **Enter**.

7. View the contents of the Student directory. Type **DIR** and press **Enter**.

8. Observe that the Config.sys file is now in the Student directory.

Renaming a file

1. Rename the Config.sys in the Student directory. Type **REN C:\STUDENT\ CONFIG.SYS C:\STUDENT\CONFIG.OLD**.

2. Observe the results, type **DIR** and press **Enter**.

5

Renaming a directory

1. Type **CD ** and press **Enter**.

2. Rename the Student directory to Student: Type **MOVE C:\STUDENT C:\STUDENT2** and press **Enter**.

3. Observe the results, type **DIR** and press **Enter**.

Viewing and changing file attributes

1. Change to the student2 directory. Type **CD STUDENT2** and press **Enter**.

2. View the attributes of the config.old. Type **ATTRIB C:\STUDENT2\CONFIG.OLD** and press **Enter**.

3. Mark the config.old file as a hidden file. Type **ATTRIB +H C:\STUDENT2\CONFIG.OLD** and press **Enter**.

4. Observe the results, type **DIR** and press **Enter**.

5. Remove the hidden attribute from the config.old file. Type **ATTRIB –H C:\STUDENT2\CONFIG.OLD** and press **Enter**.

Editing DOS configuration files

1. Type **EDIT** at the C prompt and press **Enter**.

2. Press the **Alt** key to highlight the File option in the upper left corner of the Edit program.

3. Use the down arrow on the keyboard to select the **Open** option from the File menu.

4. Press **Enter**.

5. In the Open dialog box type **C:\STUDENT2\CONFIG.OLD** and press **Enter**.

6. Press the **Alt** key to highlight the File option in the upper left corner of the Edit program.

7. Use the down arrow on the keyboard to select the **Exit** option from the File menu.

8. Press **Enter**.

Lab Notes

ATTRIB +/- H – These commands are used to set the Hidden file attribute.

ATTRIB +/- A – These commands are used to set the Archive file attribute.

ATTRIB +/- R – These commands are used to set the Read file attribute.

ATTRIB +/- S – These commands are used to set the System file attribute.

The following is a list of the files used to initialize the DOS operating system.

- MSDOS.SYS
- COMMAND.COM
- IO.SYS

These are both text files stored in the root directory and used to customize the DOS environment.

- AUTOEXEC.BAT
- CONFIG.SYS

DOS Error Messages

Incorrect DOS version – This error most commonly occurs when you try to execute a newer DOS command from an older version of DOS.

Error in CONFIG.SYS line xx – This error message will be seen during the boot process if there is an error in the CONFIG.SYS file. The xx will be the line number starting from the top of the file and counting down.

Invalid or missing COMMAND.COM – This error message will appear when COMMAND.COM is not present, is corrupt, or is the wrong version.

Remember that the DOS file naming convention includes an eight character filename and a three character file extension that is separated by a period.

Table 5-3   Dos/Windows A+ objectives

Objective	Chapters	Page Numbers
1.1 Identify the operating system's functions, structure, and major system files. Content may include the following:		
Major components of DOS, Windows 3.x and Windows 95	1, 11, 12	20-22, 547, 604-606
Major system files: what they are, where they are located and how they are used:	11	521, 524, 537, 545
System, Configuration, and User Interface files	12	628
DOS:		
Autoexec.bat	1, 2, 5	27, 67, 75, 214
Config.sys	2	66, 68-69
Io.sys	2, 4	66, 70, 148, 161
Ansi.sys	Lecture	Lecture
Msdos.sys	2, 4, 11	66, 148, 161, 580
Command.com	2, 4	67, 151, 161
1.2 Identify ways to navigate the operating system and how to get to needed technical information. Content may include the following:		
Procedures (e.g., menu or icon-driven) for navigating through DOS to perform such things as locating, accessing, and retrieving information	5	208-214
How DOS organizes and structures files in directories, Root directories, Folders and subfolders	5	201, 205-210
1.3 Identify basic concepts and procedures for creating and managing files and directories in DOS/Windows. Content may include the following:		
File naming conventions	1	13
File types, File formats	5	216-219
Command syntax	5	210-214

Table 5-3 Dos/Windows A+ objectives (continued)

Objective	Chapters	Page Numbers
1.4 Identify the procedures for viewing files and changing file attributes, and the ramifications of changes (e.g., security issues). Content may include the following:		
Use Attrib.exe	4, 5, 7	161, 165, 215, 250, 338
Read Only, Hidden, System, and Archive attributes	6, 11	322, 556
View Menu and using tabs	Discussed throughout text	Discussed throughout text
3.1 Identify the procedures for installing DOS, Windows 3.x, and Windows 95, and bringing the software to a basic operational level. Content may include the following:		
Run appropriate setup utility	11	527, 551
3.8 Identify the procedures for editing AUTOEXEC.BAT and CONFIG.SYS files.	2	68-69
4.1 Recognize and interpret the meaning of common error codes, startup messages, and icons from the boot sequence for DOS, Windows 3.x, and Windows 95. Content may include the following:		
DOS:		
Incorrect DOS version	4	165
Error in CONFIG.SYS line XX	6	322
Bad or missing Command.com	App. E, 6	322, E3
4.6 Identify the purpose of and procedures for using various DOS and Windows-based utilities and commands/switches to diagnose and troubleshoot problems. Content may include the following		
DOS:		
Edit.com	4, 7, 9	161, 338, 446, 461
Attrib.exe	4, 5	161, 165, 213, 250

REVIEW QUESTIONS

Circle True or False.

1. Using the REN command you can rename a directory. True / False

2. When you receive the error message "Invalid or missing command.com" it means that the entire operating system is corrupt and must be reinstalled. True / False

3. What does the CD command stand for?

_____

_____

_____

_____

_____

4. What is the ATTRIB command used for?

_____

_____

_____

_____

_____

5. Name one required DOS system file.

_____

_____

_____

_____

_____

6. Patrick, one of your customers, is trying to find a file on his computer which is located in the MyData directory. What command would you suggest that Patrick use to view the contents of the MyData directory?

_____

_____

_____

_____

_____

7. List the three DOS system files that are used during startup.

_____

_____

_____

_____

_____

8. John is attempting to rename his c:\Mydata directory to c:\stuff. But his computer won't let him. Describe the steps that John needs to take in order to rename the c:\Mdata directory to c:\stuff.

_____

_____

_____

_____

_____

LAB 5.4 REMOVABLE DRIVE CONFIGURATION

Objective

The objective of this lab exercise is to allow you to install a removable drive. After completing this lab exercise, you will be able to:

- Install an external removable drive.
- Name several types of removable drive technology.

Materials Required

This lab exercise requires one complete lab workstation for each group of seven students. The lab workstation should meet the following requirements:

- 486 or better
- 8MB of RAM
- 540MB or larger hard drive
- Windows 95

One removable (Zip or similar) tape drive for each group of four students

Lab Setup & Safety Tips

- To ensure complete data safety, never add or remove a removable drive while the PC is powered on.
- Each lab workstation should have Windows 95 installed and functioning properly
- The parallel port should be configured for use.

ACTIVITY

Adding a removable drive

1. Power off your lab workstation.
2. Connect the external drive to the lab workstation to the parallel port.
3. Verify that the external drive is plugged in.
4. Power on the lab workstation and allow it to boot into Windows 95.
5. Insert the driver disk for the external drive.
6. Follow the instruction for installing the drivers, or ask your instructor for details.
7. After the drivers are installed, reboot the lab workstation.
8. Test your drive installation by typing **CD** and the drive letter of the removable drive.

Lab Notes

Depending on the type of removable drive, the driver installation step will vary.

The following is a list of some commonly used external removable drives:

Iomega Zip drives

Iomega Jaz drives

Tape backup drives

SyJet drives

Magneto-optical drives

Phase-dual (PD) optical drives

Table 5-4   Core A+ objectives

Objective	Chapters	Page Numbers
1.1 Identify basic terms concepts, and functions of system modules, including how each module should work during normal operation. Examples of concepts and modules:		
Storage devices	1, 4, 5	10-11, 142, 191-249
Input devices	1, 4	2, 172, 179
Output devices	1	2
1.2 Identify basic procedures for adding and removing field replaceable modules. Examples of modules:		
Storage devices	6, 14	261-267, 733-739
Input devices	14	732
Output devices	14	732, 753

REVIEW QUESTIONS

Circle True or False.

1. Driver for external drives are always sold separately. True / False

2. External drives are always attached via a parallel port. True / False

3. Windows 95 will always automatically detect an external drive. True / False

4. Name two types of external drives.

_____

_____

_____

_____

_____

5. List several reasons you would use an external removable drive.

_____

_____

_____

_____

6. You are employed at the COMP Computer Outlet as a service technician. Bobby, one of your favorite customers, has just bought a new Zip drive and is trying to configure it. He explains to you that he is using Windows 95 and has attached his Zip drive to the proper port, but Windows will still not detect his Zip drive. List the first three questions you would ask Bobby to help discover the problem.

_____

_____

_____

_____

_____

HARD DRIVE INSTALLATION AND SUPPORT

LABS INCLUDED IN THIS CHAPTER

LAB 6.1 CONFIGURING A SINGLE HARD DRIVE SYSTEM

LAB 6.2 CONFIGURING A DUAL HARD DRIVE SYSTEM

LAB 6.1   CONFIGURING A SINGLE HARD DRIVE SYSTEM

Objective

The objective of this lab exercise is to provide you with the ability to configure one IDE hard drive when a slave is not present. After completing this lab exercise, you will be able to:

- Install and remove an IDE hard drive.

Materials Required

This lab exercise requires a minimum of one lab workstation for every four students. Each workstation should meet the following requirements:

- 486 or better
- 8MB of RAM
- One 540MB or larger IDE hard drive

One torx bit driver and any other tools necessary to open each lab workstation's case

Lab Setup & Safety Tips

- Each student must be properly grounded using a grounding mat and grounding strap. If students are working in pairs, assign Student 1 and Student 2.

- Students must comply with standard ESD procedures.

- Always unplug the power cord before touching components within the case.

ACTIVITY

Removing an IDE hard drive

Student 1

1. Power off the lab workstation and unplug the power cord (it is not necessary to unplug all cords).

2. Remove the case from the lab workstation.

3. Locate the hard drive.

4. Unplug the IDE cable and the power connector from the hard drive. Note the position of the data and power connector.

5. Use the torx bit drive or a screwdriver to dismount the hard drive.

6. Stand clear of the workstation and plug in the power cord.

7. With the hard drive removed, power on the lab workstation and wait for the BIOS error message.

8. Enter the setup program if necessary, and follow the menu instructions for the workstation's BIOS to validate the hard drive changes.

9. Save the changes and reboot the workstation.

take a picture of the computer w/o harddrive

Installing an IDE hard drive

Student 2

1. Power off the lab workstation and unplug the power cord.

2. Using the hard drive taken from Student 1's CPU, mount the hard drive in its original position.

3. Connect the IDE data cable and the power connector. (Be sure that you connect the cables in the same manner they were previously connected; the red stripe on the data cable should be aligned with the pin 1 setting on the hard drive).

4. Stand clear of the workstation and plug in the power cord.

5. When the workstation boots, enter the setup program.

6. Verify that the BIOS has automatically detected the hard drive.

7. Save the BIOS changes and exit the setup program.

8. Reboot the workstation and test the installation by booting into the operating system.

9. Shut down the workstation and power it off.

10. Unplug the power cable and secure the case.

11. Plug the workstation back in and power it on.

Lab Notes

Remember that the red stripe on an IDE data cable should always be aligned with the pin 1 on the device it is being connected to. Note: When you are connecting an IDE hard drive to an IDE data cable, the red stripe or pin one side should be attached to the same side of the hard drive as the power connector.

CERTIFICATION OBJECTIVES

Table 6-1   Core A+ objectives

Objective	Chapters	Page Numbers
1.1 Identify basic procedures for adding and removing field replaceable modules. Examples of modules:		
Storage devices	6, 14	261-267, 733-739
1.5 Identify proper procedures For installing and configuring IDE/EIDE devices. Content may Include the following:		
Master/slave	6	263, 264
Devices per channel	6	264
1.8 Recognize the functions and effective use of common hand tools. Content may include the following:		
Torx bit	7	337
Regular bit	7	337

REVIEW QUESTIONS

Circle True or False.

1. You can identify the location of pin 1 on a power connector by the red wire. True / False
2. The BIOS must be modified when the hard drive configuration has been changed. True / False
3. You should always unplug the hard drive cables while the PC is powered on. True / False
4. Hard drives are not ESD-sensitive. True / False
5. Are all IDE hard drive controllers integrated on the systemboard?

   _____

   _____

   _____

   _____

   _____

6. Donna wants to install a hard drive in her PC, but she doesn't know if she needs to buy a hard drive controller. On the lines below describe to Donna how to check and see if she will need to purchase a new hard drive controller for her computer.

   _____

   _____

   _____

   _____

   _____

LAB 6.2 CONFIGURING A DUAL HARD DRIVE SYSTEM

Objective

The objective of this lab exercise is to provide you with the experience of configuring one lab workstation to use two IDE hard drives at the same time. After completing this lab exercise, you will be able to:

- Install, remove, and configure a PC to use one or more IDE hard drives at the same time.

- Understand and describe the difference between the Cable Select and the Master/Slave configurations.

Materials Required

This lab exercise requires a minimum of one lab workstation for every four students. Each workstation should meet the following requirements:

- 486 or better
- 8MB of RAM
- Two IDE hard drives (one should already be installed in the lab workstation)

Two hard drive jumpers (normally already on the hard drives)

One grounding strap for each student

One Cable Select IDE data cable

One grounding mat for each workstation

One standard IDE data cable (Master/Slave)

One torx bit driver and any other tools necessary to open the lab workstation's case

Lab Setup & Safety Tips

- Each student must be properly grounded using a grounding mat and grounding strap. If students are working in pairs, assign Student 1 and Student 2.

- The lab workstation should be previously configured with a standard IDE data cable and one IDE hard drive set to single drive configuration.

- Students must comply with standard ESD procedures

- Always unplug the power cord before touching components within the case.

ACTIVITY

Installing a Slave drive using the Master/Slave configuration

Student 1

1. Power off the lab workstation and unplug the power cord (it is not necessary to unplug all cords).

2. Remove the case from the lab workstation.

3. Locate the hard drive.

4. Unplug the IDE cable and the power connector from the hard drive.

5. Use the torx bit driver or a screwdriver to dismount the hard drive if it is necessary to view the hard drive jumper configuration.

6. Verify that the installed hard drive is set to Master. Note: Refer to hard drive documentation for description of jumper settings.

7. Set the jumper on the second hard drive to the Slave position.

8. Locate an available bay to mount the second hard drive.

9. Mount the second hard drive.

10. Plug in the power connectors to each hard drive.

11. Plug in the IDE data cable to each hard drive.

12. Plug in the power cord and stand clear of the case.

13. With both hard drives plugged in, power on the lab workstation and wait for the BIOS error message.

14. Enter the setup program and follow the menu instructions for the workstation's BIOS to validate the hard drive changes. Note that the BIOS should now recognize two hard drives.

15. Save the changes and reboot the workstation.

16. Boot into the operating system to verify that it recognizes the additional drive.

Installing a Slave drive using Cable Select

Student 2

1. Power off the lab workstation and unplug the power cord.

2. Unplug the power connectors and the data cables of both IDE hard drives.

3. Unplug the IDE data cable from the systemboard.

4. Connect the Cable Select data cable to the systemboard in the same manner that the standard IDE data cable was connected.

   Note: The difference between a Cable Select and a standard data cable is the Cable Select data cable will be marked by a notch or a hole.

5. Change the jumper settings on both hard drives to the Cable Select position.

6. Plug in the power connectors to each of the IDE hard drives.

7. Remembering that the first hard drive on a Cable Select data cable will be the Master and the second drive will be the Slave, plug in the IDE data cables setting the original drive as Master.

8. With both hard drives plugged in, power on the lab workstation and wait for the BIOS error message.

9. Enter the setup and follow the menu instructions for the workstation's BIOS to validate the hard drive changes. Note that the BIOS should now recognize two hard drives.

10. Save the changes and reboot the workstation.

11. Boot into the operating system to verify that it recognizes the drives correctly.

12. Shut down the workstation and power it off.

13. Unplug the power cable and secure the case.

14. Plug the workstation back in and power it on.

Lab Notes

The following is a brief description of the most commonly used jumper settings:

Master – When a drive is set to Master, it will normally be the first hard drive that the PC will attempt to boot from.

Slave – When a drive is set to Slave, it will be the secondary hard drive. This drive is normally referred to as D.

Cable Select – When a drive is configured to use Cable Select, the Master/Slave designation will be determined by the drive's cable position rather than its jumper settings. Using a standard Cable Select data cable, the hard drive connected closest to the systemboard becomes the Master and the furthest drive will become the Slave.

CERTIFICATION OBJECTIVES

Table 6-2   Core A+ objectives

Objective	Chapters	Page Numbers
1.1 Identify basic procedures for adding and removing field replaceable modules. Examples of modules:		
Storage devices	6, 14	261-267, 733-739
1.5 Identify proper procedures For installing and configuring IDE/EIDE devices. Content may Include the following:		
Master/slave	6	263, 264
Devices per channel	6	264
1.8 Recognize the functions and effective use of common hand tools. Content may include the following:		
Torx bit	7	337
Regular bit	7	337

REVIEW QUESTIONS

Circle True or False.

1. When you are using Cable Select, the hard drive connected closest to the systemboard becomes the Master. True / False

2. You can add up to three devices to an IDE channel. True / False

3. When two hard drives are present, the Master drive is the drive D. True / False

4. How can you easily identify a Cable Select data cable?

_____

_____

_____

_____

_____

5. What are the three standard jumper options available with an IDE hard drive?

_____

_____

_____

_____

6. How many devices can be attached to an IDE cable?

_____

_____

_____

_____

CHAPTER SEVEN

TROUBLESHOOTING FUNDAMENTALS

LABS INCLUDED IN THIS CHAPTER

LAB 7.1 INPUT/OUTPUT DEVICE TROUBLESHOOTING

LAB 7.2 BENCHMARKING YOUR PC USING THE NUTS & BOLTS SOFTWARE

LAB 7.3 HARD DRIVE AND FLOPPY DRIVE TROUBLESHOOTING

LAB 7.4 TROUBLESHOOTING THE BOOT PROCESS

LAB 7.1 INPUT/OUTPUT DEVICE TROUBLESHOOTING

Objective

The objective of this lab exercise is to familiarize you with some of the common problems that arise during the installation of an input/output device. After completing this lab exercise, you will be able to:

- Install and configure an I/O expansion card.

- Troubleshoot the installation of an I/O expansion card.

Materials Required

This lab exercise requires one complete lab workstation for every two students. Each workstation must have one available ISA slot

One ISA I/O expansion card for each pair of students. Note that the expansion card should be jumper configurable rather than jumperless.

One screw driver and torx bit driver for each pair of students

Lab Setup & Safety Tips

- Each lab workstation should have the DOS operating system installed and functioning properly.

- Configure the I/O expansion card to utilize COM3 and COM4.

- Students must comply with standard ESD procedures.

- Always unplug the power cord before touching components within the case.

ACTIVITY

Installing the expansion card

Student 1

1. Power off the lab workstation and unplug the power cord (it is not necessary to unplug all cords).

2. Remove the case from the lab workstation.

3. Locate an available ISA slot.

4. Remove the end-of-slot blank.

5. Gently slide the ISA expansion card into the ISA slot; move the card from end to end until it is completely seated.

Warning: Do not bend the card from side to side.

6. Plug in the power cord.

7. Power on the lab workstation and enter the setup program.

8. Within the BIOS setup program, verify that the I/O expansion is recognized by your lab workstation.

9. Exit the BIOS setup program and reboot the computer.

Creating and Observing an IRQ Conflict

Student 2

1. Power off the lab workstation and remove the I/O expansion card.

2. Unplug the power cord.

3. Gently ease the I/O card out of the ISA slot.

4. Change the COM port selection jumper to COM1.

5. Gently reseat the ISA card; remember to move the card from end to end and not side to side.

6. Plug in the power cord.

7. Power on the lab workstation and observe the results.

7

Lab Notes

The type of I/O card used in this lab exercise is considered a legacy expansion card. The most commonly used I/O cards are the Plug-and-Play jumperless I/O cards.

Default IRQ setting for PC COM ports:

COM1 and **COM3** – IRQ 4

COM2 and **COM4** – IRQ 3

CERTIFICATION OBJECTIVES

Table 7-1   Core A+ objectives

Objective	Chapters	Page Numbers
1.1 Identify basic terms, concepts, and functions of system modules, including how each module should work during normal operation. Examples of concepts and modules:		
Input devices	1, 4	2, 172, 179
Output devices	1	2
BIOS	1, 2, 3	6, 56, 61, 99-105
CMOS	1, 2, 3	7, 51, 53, 120
1.2 Identify basic procedures for adding and removing field replaceable modules. Examples of modules:		
Input devices	14	732
Output devices	14	732, 753
1.3 Identify available IRQs, DMA's, and I/O addresses and procedures for configuring them for device installation, including identifying switch and jumper settings. Content may include the following:		
Standard IRQ settings	3	123
Differences between jumpers and switches	2, 8	52, 63, 388
Locating and setting switches/jumpers	2, 6, 8	53, 63, 263, 388, 403, 409

REVIEW QUESTIONS

Circle True or False.

1. COM port settings are always modified using the CMOS setup program. True / False

2. A COM port won't work properly when it is sharing an IRQ with another COM port. True / False

3. COM4 always uses IRQ 7. True / False

4. COM2 defaults to IRQ 3. True / False

5. COM stands for Communication Office Module. True / False

6. A jumperless expansion card is an expansion card without any jumpers. True / False

7. Describe how an IRQ conflict occurs.

_____

_____

_____

_____

_____

LAB 7.2 BENCHMARKING YOUR PC USING THE NUTS & BOLTS SOFTWARE

Objective

The objective of this lab exercise is to allow you the opportunity to benchmark your lab workstation. After completing this lab exercise, you should be able to:

- Benchmark a personal computer's hardware components.
- Use the Nuts & Bolts software package to run hardware diagnostics.

Materials Required

This lab will require one complete lab workstation for every two students. The lab workstation should meet the following requirements:

- 486 or better
- At least 8MB of RAM
- 540MB or larger hard drive
- CD-ROM drive

Each group of students will need to have one copy of the Nuts & Bolts software included with the textbook.

Lab Setup & Safety Tips

- Each lab workstation should have the Nuts & Bolts software installed and functioning properly.

ACTIVITY

Benchmarking your CPU

1. Power on your lab workstation and allow it to boot into Windows 95.

2. Click the **Start** button.

3. Click the **Nuts & Bolts** icon.

4. Click the **Discover** icon.

5. Click **Category**.

6. Select **System** on the Category menu.

7. Double-click the **CPU info.** icon.

8. Record the following information about your CPU:

Model _____

Stepping _____

L1 cache _____

L2 cache _____

Speed in MHZ _____

Benchmarking your hard drive

1. Click the **Start** button.

2. Click the **Nuts & Bolts** icon.

3. Click the **Discover** icon.

4. Click **Category**.

5. Select **Benchmark** on the Category menu.

6. Double-click the **HD Benchmark** icon.

7. Select your drive C by clicking on it.

8. Click the **Run benchmark** button.

9. Record the following:

   Transfer rates MB/Sec _____

   Average seek time Msec _____

Running diagnostics

1. Click the **Start** button.

2. Click the **Nuts & Bolts** icon.

3. Click the **Discover** icon.

4. Click **Category**.

5. Select **Diagnostic** on the Category menu.

6. Double-click the **Summary Diag.** icon.

7. Observe the results.

Lab Notes

What is Nuts & Bolts? – The Nuts & Bolts software that is included with your textbook is a third-party software package designed to help you troubleshoot and benchmark your PC.

CERTIFICATION OBJECTIVES

Table 7-2   Core A+ objectives

Objective	Chapters	Page Numbers
1.10 Identify hardware methods of system optimization and when to use them. Content may include the following:		
Memory	11	527
Hard Drives	5, 11	221, 545
CPU	3	89, 118
Cache memory	9	432
2.2 Identify basic troubleshooting procedures and good practices for eliciting problem symptoms from customers. Content may include the following:		
Troubleshooting/isolation/problem determination procedures	7	345
Determine whether hardware or software problem	7	349

REVIEW QUESTIONS

Circle True or False.

1. L1 cache and L2 cache are both housed within the CPU. True / False

2. The Nuts & Bolts software always uses a diagnostic card to test a PC's components. True / False

3. The hard drive seek time is the amount of time it takes your hard drive to locate a particular data cluster. True / False

4. Describe how you could use the Nuts & Bolts software to identify if a problem is hardware or software related.

_____

_____

_____

_____

_____

7

LAB 7.3 HARD DRIVE AND FLOPPY DRIVE TROUBLESHOOTING

Objective

The objective of this lab exercise is to allow you time to develop hard drive and floppy drive troubleshooting skills. After completing this lab exercise, you should be able to:

- Troubleshoot all types of PC floppy drive configurations.
- Troubleshoot all types of PC hard drive configurations.
- Describe and implement the troubleshooting process.

Materials Required

This lab will require one complete lab workstation for every four students. The lab workstations should meet the following requirements:

- 486 or better
- At least 8MB of RAM
- 540MB or larger hard drive

Lab Setup & Safety Tips

- Each lab workstation should have Windows 95 installed and functioning properly.

ACTIVITY

Creating problem 1

Student 1

While Student 2 is away from the lab workstation, proceed with the following steps:

1. Power off the lab workstation and unplug the power cord (it is not necessary to unplug all cords).

2. Remove the case from the lab workstation.

3. Locate the hard drive.

4. Unplug the IDE cable and the power connector from the hard drive.

5. Replace the case.

6. Plug in the power cord.

Troublshooting and resolving problem 1

Student 2

After Student 1 has reconfigured the lab workstation, answer the following questions and repair the lab workstation.

Are there any error messages? If so, write them down.

_____

_____

_____

_____

What is the problem (be specific)?

_____

_____

_____

_____

_____

List several possible solutions.

_____

_____

_____

_____

_____

Test your theory (solution) and record the results.

_____

_____

_____

_____

_____

How did you discover the problem?

_____

_____

_____

_____

_____

What could you do differently next time to improve your troubleshooting process?

_____

_____

_____

_____

_____

Creating problem 2

Student 2

While Student 1 is away from the lab workstation, proceed with the following steps:

1. Power off the lab workstation and unplug the power cord (it is not necessary to unplug all cords).

2. Remove the case from the lab workstation.

3. Locate the floppy drive.

4. Unplug the floppy drive data cable.

5. Using the incorrect connector on the data cable, plug the floppy drive into the data cable.

6. Replace the case.

7. Plug in the power cord.

Troubleshooting and resolving problem 2

Student 1

After Student 2 has reconfigured the lab workstation, answer the following questions and repair the lab workstation.

Are there any error messages? If so, write them down.

_____

_____

_____

_____

_____

What is the problem (be specific)?

_____

_____

_____

_____

List several possible solutions.

_____

_____

_____

_____

Test your theory (solution) and record the results.

_____

_____

_____

_____

How did you discover the problem?

_____

_____

_____

_____

What could you do differently next time to improve your troubleshooting process?

_____

_____

_____

_____

Lab Notes

The six steps of the troubleshooting process –

1. Let the customer explain the problem.

2. Search for answers.

3. Develop a hypothesis.

4. Test your theory.

5. Resolve the problem and explain your changes to the customer.

6. Complete proper documentation.

What is troubleshooting documentation? – Troubleshooting documentation includes any sort of documenting required by your employer and/or your own collection of notes and files.

7

CERTIFICATION OBJECTIVES

Table 7-3   Core A+ objectives

Objective	Chapters	Page Numbers
2.1 Identify common symptoms and problems associated with each module and how to troubleshoot and isolate the problems. Content may include the following:		
Hard Drives	App. E, 6	E4, 313, 324
POST audible/visual error codes	App. A	A1
2.2 Identify basic troubleshooting procedures and good practices for eliciting problem symptoms from customers. Content may include the following:		
Troubleshooting/isolation/problem determination procedures	7	345
Determine whether hardware or software problem	7	349
Symptoms/Error Codes	App. E	E1
Situation when the problem occurred	18	946

REVIEW QUESTIONS

Circle True or False.

1. You should always verify that your sound card is functioning properly before troubleshooting a hard drive problem. True / False

2. While you are troubleshooting a problem, it is best to only make one change at a time. True / False

3. List three of the six troubleshooting steps below.

_____

_____

_____

_____

4. Describe how a floppy drive will behave if it is not plugged in correctly.

_____

_____

_____

_____

LAB 7.4 TROUBLESHOOTING THE BOOT PROCESS

Objective

The objective of this lab exercise is to allow you time to further develop your troubleshooting skills and master the PC boot process. After completing this lab exercise, you should be able to:

- Successfully troubleshoot all types of PC configurations.

- Describe and implement the troubleshooting process, and explain how it pertains to the PC boot process.

Materials Required

This lab will require one complete lab workstation for every four students. The lab workstations should meet the following requirements:

- 486 or better
- At least 8MB of RAM
- 540MB or larger hard drive
- CD-ROM drive

Lab Setup & Safety Tips

- Each lab workstation should have Windows 95 installed and functioning properly.

ACTIVITY

Creating problem 1

Student 1

While Student 2 is away from the lab workstation, proceed with the following steps:

1. Power off the lab workstation and unplug the power cord (it is not necessary to unplug all cords).

2. Remove the case from the lab workstation.

3. Unplug the P8 and P9 connectors from the systemboard.

4. Replace the case.

5. Plug in the power cord.

Troubleshooting and resolving problem 1

Student 2

After Student 1 has reconfigured the lab workstation, answer the following questions and repair the lab workstation.

Are there any error messages? If so, write them down.

_____

_____

_____

_____

_____

What is the problem (be specific)?

_____

_____

_____

_____

_____

List several possible solutions.

_____

_____

_____

_____

_____

Test your theory (solution) and record the results.

_____

_____

_____

_____

_____

How did you discover the problem?

_____

_____

_____

_____

_____

What could you do differently next time to improve your troubleshooting process?

_____

_____

_____

_____

_____

Creating problem 2

Student 2

While Student 1 is away from the lab workstation, proceed with the following steps:

1. Power off the lab workstation and unplug the power cord (it is not necessary to unplug all cords).

2. Remove the case from the lab workstation.

3. Locate the hard drive.

4. Move the jumper of the hard drive to the Slave position.

5. Replace the case.

6. Plug in the power cord.

Troubleshooting and resolving problem 2

Student 1

After Student 2 has reconfigured the lab workstation, answer the following questions and repair the lab workstation.

Are there any error messages? If so, write them down.

_____

_____

_____

_____

_____

What is the problem (be specific)?

_____

_____

_____

_____

List several possible solutions.

_____

_____

_____

_____

Test your theory (solution) and record the results.

_____

_____

_____

_____

How did you discovery the problem?

_____

_____

_____

_____

What could you do differently next time to improve your troubleshooting process?

_____

_____

_____

_____

Lab Notes

Which way should the P8 and P9 connectors be attached? – When connecting the P8 and P9 power connectors, remember that the ground or the black wires should always face each other.

How do I improve my troubleshooting skills? – Troubleshooting is a skill that takes time and experience to develop. Exercises like this one will help you improve your troubleshooting skills by allowing you to have that experience without the pressure of your customer's expectations. When you see a new error message, rather than avoiding the problem, become the relentless investigator and search for the answer. Your troubleshooting skills and experiences will grow exponentially from the process of your investigation.

CERTIFICATION OBJECTIVES

7

Table 7-4   Core A+ objectives

Objective	Chapters	Page Numbers
2.1 Identify common symptoms and problems associated with each module and how to troubleshoot and isolate the problems. Content may include the following:		
Hard Drives	App. E, 6	E4, 313, 324
POST audible/visual error codes	App. A	A1
2.2 Identify basic troubleshooting procedures and good practices for eliciting problem symptoms from customers. Content may include the following:		
Troubleshooting/isolation/problem determination procedures	7	345
Determine whether hardware or software problem	7	349
Symptoms/Error Codes	App. E	E1
Situation when the problem occurred	18	946

REVIEW QUESTIONS

Circle True or False.

1. Always ask the customer to leave when you are going to troubleshoot a PC. True / False

2. Asking the customer questions can almost always help you resolve their issue faster. True / False

3. If a problem is detected during POST the BIOS will normally return an error message. True / False

4. Describe the symptoms of an unplugged hard drive.

_____

_____

_____

_____

CUSTOMIZING A PERSONAL COMPUTER SYSTEM WITH PERIPHERAL EQUIPMENT

LABS INCLUDED IN THIS CHAPTER

LAB 8.1 SERIAL PORT CONFLICT RESOLUTION

Objective

Serial port conflicts commonly occur when an internal modem is installed into a PC. You can approach troubleshooting these sorts of conflicts in several different ways, depending on the environment. This lab exercise will show you how to properly troubleshoot a serial port conflict in the Windows 95 environment. After completing this lab exercise, you will be able to:

- Define a serial port conflict.
- Describe the symptoms of a serial port conflict.
- Use the Device Manager to discover which device is conflicting with the serial port.
- Resolve serial port conflicts.

Materials Required

This lab exercise requires one complete lab workstation for every four students. The lab workstation should meet the following requirements:

- 486 or better
- 8MB of RAM
- Windows 95
- One jumpered internal modem including documentation for the internal modem's jumper settings (phone line is not necessary)
- At least one COM port

One ESD mat for each lab workstation

Grounding straps for each student

Lab Setup & Safety Tips

- Each lab workstation should have Windows 95 installed and functioning properly.
- Each lab workstation should have an internal modem installed and functioning properly.
- Each lab workstation's modem should be configured to use COM2.
- Each lab workstation's COM port should be configured to use COM1.

ACTIVITY

Creating and observing the conflict

1. Power off the lab workstation.

2. Unplug the power cord.

3. Remove the case from the lab workstation.

4. Locate the modem.

5. Using the provided documentation, change the modem jumper settings from COM2 to COM1.

6. Replace the case and plug in the power cord.

7. Power on your lab workstation and allow it to boot into Windows 95. Note that depending on the type of system, you may receive an error message during the POST. Observe the error message and continue booting the system by following the instructions on the screen.

8. Click the **Start** button, point to **Settings**, then click **Control Panel**.

9. Double-click the **System** icon.

10. Click the **Device Manager** tab.

11. Look for yellow exclamation points located on top of COM1 and the modem icon. If the yellow exclamation marks now exist over the modem and COM1, then you have successfully created a resource conflict between the two devices.

Resolving the conflict

There are several different ways to resolve this conflict, the best answer really depends on the needs of the user. For example, you already know that you can easily resolve this conflict by simply changing the modem jumper settings back to their original settings. Another solution would be to disable or reassign the COM port's resources.

Reassigning or disabling the COM port's resources

1. Reboot your lab workstation.

2. Enter the BIOS setup program.

3. Locate the serial configuration section.

4. Change your serial port configuration from COM2 to Disabled.

5. Save the changes and reboot the lab workstation.

Note: Not all serial ports are configurable through the BIOS. If the COM port configuration is not available through the BIOS setup program of your lab workstation, ask your instructor for I/O card configuration.

Lab Notes

Table 8-1   Default port assignments on many computers

Port	IRQ	Type	I/O Address
COM1	IRQ 4	Serial	03F8
COM2	IRQ 3	Serial	02F8
COM3	IRQ 4	Serial	03E8
COM4	IRQ 3	Serial	02E8
LPT1:	IRQ 7	Parallel	0378
LPT2:	IRQ 5	Parallel	0278

Note that in some of the more severe cases, a PC will completely freeze when a serial port conflict occurs.

Viewing device resources – You can use the Device Manager to view resource settings by simply double-clicking the device icon.

Yellow exclamation marks in the Device Manager? – When the Device Manager displays a yellow exclamation mark over a device, it means that the device is conflicting with another device.

A red "X" in the Device Manager? – When the Device Manger displays a red "X" over a device, this means that the device has been disabled in the current hardware profile.

CERTIFICATION OBJECTIVES

Table 8-2 Core A+ objectives

Objective	Chapters	Page Numbers
1.1 Identify basic terms, concepts, and functions of system modules, including how each module should work during normal operation. Examples of concepts and modules:		
Modem	1, 15	8, 763
Input devices	1, 4	2, 172, 179
Output devices	1	2
2.1 Identify common symptoms and problems associated with each module and how to troubleshoot and isolate the problems. Content may include the following:		
Modems	15	796-799
POST audible/visual error codes	App. A	A1
2.2 Identify basic troubleshooting procedures and good practices for eliciting problem symptoms from customers. Content may include the following:		
Troubleshooting/isolation/problem determination procedures	7	345
4.4 Identify the purpose of CMOS (Complementary Metal-Oxide Semiconductor), what it contains and how to change its basic parameters. Example Basic CMOS Settings:		
Com/serial port – memory address, interrupt request, disable	1, 3	7, 51, 120-121

Table 8-3 DOS/Windows A+ objectives

Objective	Chapters	Page Numbers
4.5 Recognize and categorize common problems and identify what could cause them. Content may include the following:		
System lock up	11	529
4.6 Identify the purpose of and procedures for using various DOS and Windows-based utilities and commands/switches to diagnose and troubleshoot problems. Content may include the following:		
Windows-based tools:		
Device manager	1, 8	37, 410-411
Control Panel	12	625

REVIEW QUESTIONS

Circle True or False.

1. The Device Manager can be found by opening the Control Panel and then clicking the Network icon. True / False

2. A red "X" in the Device Manager means that the device is disabled. True / False

3. All serial ports can be configured using the BIOS setup program. True / False

4. Serial ports can only conflict with modems. True / False

5. What IRQ does COM4 normally use?

_____

_____

_____

_____

_____

6. Describe how to view the IRQ of a device using the Device Manager.

_____

_____

_____

_____

_____

7. List two ways of resolving a serial conflict.

_____

_____

_____

_____

_____

8. You are the desktop PC support technician for the Good Job Corporation. Janet, one of your customers, suspects that she has a resource conflict between her newly installed modem and one of her serial ports on her laptop. Describe how you could use the Device Manager to confirm or eliminate her suspicions.

_____

_____

_____

_____

_____

9. Steve, one of your customers, has just installed an I/O card into his PC because he needed more than two COM ports. He is now receiving an error message every time he starts his system. Steve has asked you to troubleshoot. Describe the steps you would take to resolve Steve's conflict.

_____

_____

_____

_____

_____

LAB 8.2 PARALLEL PORT CONFLICT RESOLUTION

Objective

Parallel port conflicts commonly occur when a sound card is installed into a PC. In this lab exercise you will examine the process of locating and resolving a parallel port conflict. After completing this lab exercise, you will be able to:

- Define a parallel port conflict.
- Describe the symptoms of a parallel port conflict.
- Use the Device Manager to discover which device is conflicting with a parallel port.
- Resolve parallel port conflicts.

Materials Required

This lab exercise requires one complete lab workstation for every four students. The lab workstations should meet the following requirements:

- 486 or better
- 8MB of RAM
- Windows 95
- One 8 or 16-bit sound card
- At least one LPT port

One ESD mat

Grounding straps for each student

Documentation containing your sound card's jumper settings

Lab Setup & Safety Tips

- Each lab workstation should have Windows 95 installed and functioning properly.
- Each lab workstation should have a sound card installed and functioning properly.
- Each lab workstation's sound card should be configured to use IRQ 5.
- LPT1 should be configured to use default settings.

ACTIVITY

Creating and Observing the conflict

1. Power off the lab workstation.

2. Unplug the power cord.

3. Remove the case from the lab workstation.

4. Locate the sound card.

5. Using the provided documentation, change the sound card jumper settings from IRQ 5 to IRQ 7.

6. Replace the case and plug in the power cord.

7. Power on your lab workstation and allow it to boot to Windows 95. Note that depending on the type of system, you may receive an error message during the POST. Observe the error message and continue to boot the system by following the instructions on the screen.

8. Click the **Start** button, point to **Settings**, then click **Control Panel**.

9. Double-click the **System** icon.

10. Click the **Device Manager** tab.

11. Look for yellow exclamation points located on top of LPT1 and the sound card icon. If the yellow exclamation marks exist over the sound card and LPT1, then you have successfully created a resource conflict between the two devices.

Resolving the Conflict

There are several different ways to resolve a parallel port conflict. Like serial conflicts, a parallel conflict can also be resolved by simply disabling the parallel port. Under normal circumstances however, you will not be allowed to disable the parallel port because the user will need to use it for their printer. This leaves you with two options. One is to reassign the resources of the conflicting device, and the other is to reassign the resources of the parallel port.

Reassigning or disabling the parallel port's resources

1. Reboot your lab workstation.

2. Enter the BIOS setup program.

3. Locate the parallel configuration section.

4. Change your parallel port resources settings to IRQ 5, and be sure to use a different I/O address.

5. Save the changes and reboot the lab workstation.

Verifying the resource conflict has been resolved

1. Power on your lab workstation and allow it to boot into Windows 95.

2. Click the **Start** button, point to **Settings**, then click **Control Panel**.

3. Double-click the **System** icon.

4. Click the **Device Manager** tab.

5. Double-click **Ports**.

6. Double-click **LPT1**.

7. Click the **Resources** tab.

Note that the IRQ and I/O settings now read what you have previously chosen in the BIOS setup program.

8. Click the **Cancel** button.

9. Double-click **Sound, video,** and **game controllers**.

10. Double-click the **sound card** icon.

11. Click the **Resources** tab.

12. Observe the IRQ and I/O settings of the sound card.

Note: Not all parallel ports are configurable through the BIOS. If the parallel port configuration is not available through the BIOS setup program of your lab workstation, ask your instructor for the proper configuration.

8

Lab Notes

COM port assignment vs. LPT assignment – Unlike COM ports, parallel ports do not allow you to simply change the LPT number from LPT1 to LPT2 and maintain the same system resources. The difference is, a COM port number (1, 2, 3, 4) can be assigned any I/O address and IRQ that are reserved for COM use. However, a parallel port is assigned its LPT number (1, 2, 3) by the BIOS in the order of highest I/O address first.

Parallel ports only work on printers? – Parallel communication was originally intended for use with printers only. But because parallel port communication is faster than serial communication, it is commonly used for fast data transfers over short distances. To accomplish this sort of data transfer a *bi-directional* parallel port is used.

Note that in some of the more severe cases, a PC will completely freeze when a parallel port conflict occurs.

CERTIFICATION OBJECTIVES

Table 8-4 Core A+ objectives

Objective	Chapters	Page Numbers
1.1 Identify basic terms, concepts, and functions of system modules, including how each module should work during normal operation. Examples of concepts and modules:		
Input devices	1, 4	2, 172, 179
Output devices	1	2
1.3 Identify available IRQs, DMA's, and I/O addresses and procedures for configuring them for device installation, including identifying switch and jumper settings. Content may include the following:		
Standard IRQ settings	3	123
Differences between jumpers and switches	2, 6	52, 263
Locating and setting switches/jumpers	2, 6, 8	52, 63, 263, 388, 403, 409
Sound Cards	8	385, 386
1.4 Identify common peripheral ports, associated cabling, and their connectors. Content may include the following:		
Serial versus parallel	8, 14	393, 732
2.1 Identify common symptoms and problems associated with each module and how to troubleshoot and isolate the problems. Content may include the following:		
Parallel Ports/scanners/tape drives	7	357
Sound Card/Audio	13	687
POST audible/visual error codes	App. A	A1
4.4 Identify the purpose of CMOS (Complementary Metal-Oxide Semiconductor), what it contains and how to change its basic parameters. Example Basic CMOS Settings:		
Printer parallel port - Uni., bi-directional, disable/enable, ECP, EPP	14	748-751

REVIEW QUESTIONS

Circle True or False.

1. Parallel ports are assigned their LPT number by the BIOS. True / False

2. Parallel ports do not need an IRQ. True / False

3. You can only have one parallel port per computer. True / False

4. Serial ports commonly conflict with parallel ports. True / False

5. Describe how to view the IRQ of a device using the Device Manager.

   _____

   _____

   _____

   _____

   _____

6. Briefly describe how parallel ports are assigned LPT numbers.

   _____

   _____

   _____

   _____

   _____

7. List two ways a parallel port conflict can be resolved.

   _____

   _____

   _____

   _____

   _____

8. You are working on a PC that has the parallel port built into the systemboard. You are about to install a new sound card that will use IRQ 7. Describe the steps you will need to take to avoid an IRQ conflict with the sound card.

   _____

   _____

   _____

   _____

   _____

LAB 8.3 SCSI ADAPTER INSTALLATION

Objective

The objective of this lab exercise is to allow you the opportunity to properly install, and configure a SCSI host adapter. After completing this lab exercise, you will be able to:

- Properly install a SCSI, host adapter.

- Describe several different ways SCSI host adapters are utilized.

- Use the Device Manager to view a SCSI host adapters resources.

- Describe the difference between the SCSI BIOS setup program and the system CMOS setup program.

Materials Required

This lab exercise requires one complete lab workstation for every four students. The lab workstations should meet the following requirements:

- 486 or better
- 8MB of RAM
- Windows 95

One SCSI host adapter for each lab workstation

One ESD mat

Grounding straps for each student

Several disks containing the necessary Windows 95 drivers for each SCSI card

Documentation containing your SCSI card's jumper settings

Lab Setup & Safety Tips

- The instructor will provide the students with the proper resource settings for their lab workstations.

- Each lab workstation should have Windows 95 installed and functioning properly.

- Students must comply with standard ESD procedures.

- Always unplug the power cord before touching components within the case.

ACTIVITY

Installing the SCSI Host Adapter

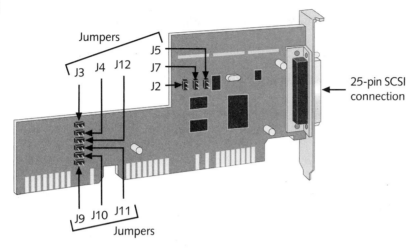

Figure 8-1 SCSI host adapter for one single-ended device

1. Power off the lab workstation.

2. Unplug the power cord.

3. Remove the case from the lab workstation.

4. Locate an available expansion slot for your SCSI host adapter.

5. Using the provided documentation, verify that your SCSI card is configured to your instructor's resource specifications.

6. Replace the case and plug in the power cord.

7. Power on your lab workstation and allow it to boot to Windows 95.

8. While Windows 95 is booting, watch to see if it automatically detects the new SCSI card.

If Windows 95 detects the SCSI card and prompts you for the drivers

1. Insert the driver disk.

2. Click the **Drivers provided by the hardware manufacturer** option button.

3. Click the **OK** button.

4. Use the Browse button to locate the drivers on the disk.

5. Click **OK**.

6. Select the driver for the SCSI card that you installed.

7. Click **OK**.

8. If you are prompted for the Windows 95 cab files, use the Browse button to locate them.

If Windows 95 does not detect the SCSI card

1. Click the **Start** button, point to **Settings**, then click **Control Panel**.

2. Double-click the **Add New hardware** icon.

3. Click the **Next** button three times to allow Windows 95 to detect the SCSI card.

4. Install the driver from the disk when prompted.

Verifying the SCSI host adapter driver installation

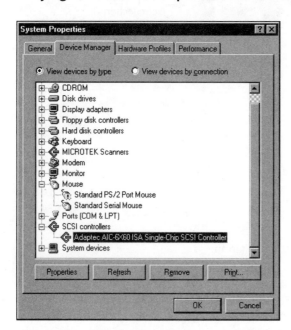

Figure 8-2   Device Manager displays the newly installed host adapter

1. Click the **Start** button, point to **Settings**, then click **Control Panel**.

2. Double-click on the **System** icon.

3. Click the **Device Manager** tab.

4. Double-click the **SCSI Controllers** icon.

5. Verify that the SCSI host adapter driver is properly installed without any errors (there shouldn't be any yellow exclamation marks).

Viewing the SCSI setup program

1. Reboot your lab workstation.

   After the standard system POST is complete, you should see a SCSI BIOS screen.

2. Following the directions on the SCSI BIOS screen, enter the SCSI CMOS setup program.

3. Follow the direction for the SCSI BIOS and observe the different options.

Lab Notes

Different types of SCSI host adapters – There are several different types of SCSI host adapters ranging from single proprietary host adapters to larger scale host adapters that can support many SCSI devices. Following is an example of a SCSI device designed to support on external SCSI device.

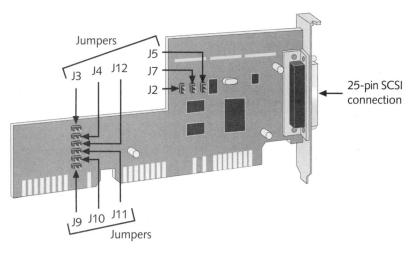

Figure 8-3   SCSI host adapter for one single-ended device

8

Configuring a PC to use both IDE and SCSI hard drives – Configuring a PC to use both an IDE and a SCSI hard drive at the same time is relatively simple. First, configure the IDE drive as Master. Second, configure the SCSI drive to use an available SCSI ID. You must always remember that on a PC with both IDE and SCSI, the IDE drive must be drive C; this is because the system BIOS loads before the SCSI BIOS.

What is the difference between SCSI and IDE? – One of the most important differences between SCSI and IDE is that the SCSI is substantially faster than IDE.

CERTIFICATION OBJECTIVES

Table 8-5   Core A+ objectives

Objective	Chapters	Page Numbers
1.6 Identify proper procedures for installing and configuring SCSI devices. Content may include the following:		
Internal versus external	8	408, 409
Switch and jumper settings	6	275

Table 8-6   DOS/Windows A+ objectives

Objective	Chapters	Page Numbers
3.2 Identify steps to perform an operating system upgrade. Content may include the following:		
Loading drivers	8, 11	389-391, 544
3.4 Identify how Windows 95 uses plug and play, and how it functions. Content may include the following:		
BIOS/OS recognizes peripherals and loads appropriate drivers and assigns system resources	11	562, 563
When working properly	11	563
When not working properly	11	564, 568

REVIEW QUESTIONS

Circle True or False.

1. SCSI is faster than IDE. True / False

2. To install a SCSI host adapter on a PC, there must be one available IRQ. True / False

3. All SCSI hard drives have a built-in BIOS. True / False

4. You can modify the SCSI BIOS through the system BIOS. True / False

5. When a PC is configured to use both SCSI and IDE, which drive must be drive C, and why?

   _____

   _____

   _____

   _____

   _____

6. You are working employed as a desktop PC support technician at the Black Moon Company. Carol, one of your customers, has asked that you install a SCSI host adapter into her computer. Describe the steps necessary to complete the job Carol has asked you to do.

   _____

   _____

   _____

   _____

   _____

LAB 8.4 SCSI CHAIN CONFLICT RESOLUTION

Objective

The objective of this lab exercise is to allow you the opportunity to troubleshoot and resolve a SCSI chain conflict. After completing this lab exercise, you will be able to:

- Describe how a SCSI chain conflict occurs.
- Install and configure a SCSI hard drive.
- Properly identify a SCSI chain conflict.
- Resolve a SCSI chain conflict.

Materials Required

This lab exercise requires one complete lab workstation for every four students. The lab workstations should meet the following requirements:

- 486 or better
- 8MB of RAM
- Windows 95
- One SCSI host adapter installed

Two SCSI hard drives for each lab workstation

One ESD mat

Grounding straps for each student

Documentation for the each SCSI hard drive jumper configuration

Lab Setup & Safety Tips

- Each lab workstation should have Windows 95 installed and functioning properly.
- Students must comply with standard ESD procedures.
- Always unplug the power cord before touching components within the case.
- One SCSI hard drive should be properly installed and configured prior to starting the lab exercise.
- The previously installed IDE hard drive should be configured as drive C and contain the operating system.

ACTIVITY

Creating the SCSI chain conflict

For the purpose of this lab exercise, the installed SCSI hard drive will be referred to as SCSI drive. The second SCSI hard drive, used to create the conflict, will be referred to as SCSI drive 2.

1. Power off the lab workstation.
2. Unplug the power cord.
3. Remove the case from the lab workstation.
4. Using the jumper documentation provided, set the two SCSI hard drives to the same SCSI ID.
5. Mount SCSI drive 2.

6. Plug in the power and data cables to SCSI drive 2.

7. Stand clear of the case and plug in the power cord.

8. Power on your lab workstation and allow it to boot into Windows 95.

9. Observe the error messages during the boot process.

Resolving the SCSI chain conflict

1. Power off the lab workstation.

2. Unplug the power cord.

3. Locate SCSI drive 2.

4. Dismount SCSI drive 2.

5. Unplug the power and data cables.

6. Using the jumper documentation provided, set SCSI drive 2 to an available SCSI ID.

7. Mount SCSI drive 2.

8. Plug in the power and data cables to SCSI drive 2.

9. Replace the case and plug in the power cord.

10. Power on the lab workstation and enter the SCSI BIOS setup program.

11. Verify that the SCSI BIOS recognizes both SCSI drives correctly.

12. Exit the setup program and reboot the lab workstation.

13. Allow your lab workstation to boot into Windows 95.

14. Double-click the **My Computer** icon.

15. Verify that Windows 95 recognizes both SCSI hard drives.

Lab Notes

What is SCAM? – SCAM stands for SCSI configuration automatically. It is a method in which SCSI devices and the host adapter are Plug-and–Play-compliant, and the user does not need to manually set the ID on the device.

What is termination all about? – SCSI devices require some sort of termination to prevent signal bounce. There are several different types of terminators available. Each of these terminators vary in quality and compatibility. Some devices are self-terminating. Consult your SCSI host adapter documentation for the proper termination specifications.

CERTIFICATION OBJECTIVES

Table 8-7   Core A+ objectives

Objective	Chapters	Page Numbers
1.6 Identify proper procedures for installing and configuring SCSI devices. Content may include the following:		
Address/Termination conflicts	5, 6	240, 275
Cabling Types (example: regular, wide, ultra-wide)	5	240-243
Switch and jumper settings	6	275

Table 8-8   DOS/Windows A+ objectives

Objective	Chapters	Page Numbers
3.2 Identify steps to perform an operating system upgrade. Content may include the following:		
Loading drivers	8, 11	389-391, 544
3.4 Identify how Windows 95 uses plug and play, and how it functions. Content may include the following:		
BIOS/OS recognizes peripherals and loads appropriate drivers and assigns system resources	11	562, 563
When working properly	11	563
When not working properly	11	564, 568

REVIEW QUESTIONS

Circle True or False.

1. A SCSI chain conflict occurs when a SCSI device is not plugged into the SCSI cable. True / False

2. A SCSI chain conflict occurs when two or more SCSI drives are set to Master. True / False

3. All SCSI standards require some sort of termination. True / False

4. SCAM stands for SCSI Configuration Automatically. True / False

5. How is SCAM helpful?

_____

_____

_____

_____

_____

6. You are working employed as a desktop PC support technician at the Black Moon Company. Bob, one of your customers, wants you to write him directions for installing and configuring a SCSI hard drive. Write the instructions you would give to Bob.

_____

_____

_____

_____

_____

8

UNDERSTANDING AND MANAGING MEMORY

LABS INCLUDED IN THIS CHAPTER

LAB 9.1 INSTALLING RAM AND UNDERSTANDING THE CONFIG.SYS

LAB 9.2 MEMORY MANAGEMENT IN DOS AND WINDOWS 3.x

LAB 9.3 MEMORY MANAGEMENT IN WINDOWS 95

LAB 9.4 MEMORY MANAGEMENT IN WINDOWS NT

LAB 9.1 INSTALLING RAM AND UNDERSTANDING THE CONFIG.SYS

Objective

The objective of this lab exercise is to teach you how to properly install RAM and to understand the differences between the different kinds of RAM currently sold on the market. After completing this lab exercise you will be able to:

- Install RAM.

- Write and modify a CONFIG.SYS file.

- Describe features of different types of RAM.

Materials Required

This lab exercise requires one complete lab workstation for every four students. The lab workstation should meet the following requirements:

- 486 or better
- 4MB of RAM
- Windows 95
- One 4MB or larger RAM chip

One ESD mat for each lab workstation

Grounding straps for each student

Lab Setup & Safety Tips

- Each lab workstation should have both Windows 95 and DOS 5.0 or greater installed and functioning properly.

- Students must comply with standard ESD procedures.

- Always unplug the power cord before touching components within the case.

ACTIVITY

Installing RAM

1. Power off the lab workstation.

2. Unplug the power cord.

3. Remove the case from the lab workstation.

4. Locate the SIMM banks on your systemboard.

5. Place the SIMM at a 45-degree angle and then gently snap into place.

6. After the SIMM has been installed, replace the case.

7. Plug in the power cord.

8. Power on your lab workstation.

9. Enter the CMOS setup program.

10. Verify that the setup program recognizes the correct amount of memory.

11. Save the changes and reboot the workstation.

12. Allow you lab workstation to boot into Windows 95.

13. Right-click the **My Computer** icon.

14. Select **Properties** from the menu.

15. On the General tab, locate the Computer heading.

16. Verify that Windows 95 is utilizing all of the installed memory.

Recording the different characteristics of RAM

In the following section write the definition for each type of RAM; be sure to include how it is used and any advantages or disadvantages. You will find the definitions in the textbook on pages 430 through 436.

SRAM _____

_____

_____

_____

_____

DRAM _____

_____

_____

_____

_____

DIMMS _____

_____

_____

_____

_____

Parity RAM _____

_____

_____

_____

_____

Nonparity RAM _____

_____

_____

_____

_____

EDO RAM _____

_____

_____

_____

_____

9

FPM RAM _____

_____

_____

_____

_____

Flash Memory _____

_____

_____

_____

_____

SDRAM _____

_____

_____

_____

_____

COAST _____

_____

_____

_____

_____

Examining the CONFIG.SYS

1. Allow your lab workstation to boot to DOS.

2. Type **EDIT CONFIG.SYS** and press **Enter**. Your lab workstation should respond by launching the EDIT program and opening the your CONFIG.SYS file.

On the lines below copy the contents of your CONFIG.SYS; then next to each command, write how your lab workstation should respond. You will find the definition in the textbook on pages 445 through 456.

Example:

BUFFERS=40 – This command tells DOS how many buffers to maintain when transferring data to and from secondary storage.

_____

_____

_____

_____

_____

_____

_____

_____

_____

_____

_____

_____

_____

_____

_____

_____

_____

_____

_____

_____

_____

_____

_____

Lab Notes

What is conventional memory? – Conventional memory, or base memory, is the first 640K of RAM.

What is upper memory? – Upper memory includes memory addresses starting at 641K and up to 1024K.

What is extended memory? – Memory addresses above 1024K are referred to as residing in extended memory.

What is expanded memory? – Expanded memory is memory that falls outside of the linear memory addressing scheme. Note that expanded memory is normally accessed via upper memory. Refer to textbook page 442 for more about expanded memory.

What is virtual memory? – Virtual memory is an area for secondary storage set aside to be used as an area of RAM. Note that because it is secondary storage the access time is considerable slower than that of RAM.

CERTIFICATION OBJECTIVES

Table 9-1   Core A+ objectives

Objective	Chapters	Page Numbers
4.2 Identify the categories of RAM (Random Access Memory) terminology, their locations, and physical characteristics. Content may include the following: Terminology:		
EDO RAM (Extended Data Output RAM)	3, 9	106, 434
DRAM (Dynamic Random Access Memory)	1, 9	6-7, 430
SRAM (Static RAM)	3, 9	107, 430, 435
Locations and physical characteristics: Memory bank	9	431
Memory chips (8 bit, 16 bit, and 32 bit)	9	430-436
SIMMS (Single In-line Memory Module)	3, 9	106, 432, 474
DIMMS (Dual In-line Memory Module)	3, 9	106, 432, 474
Parity chips versus non-parity chips	3, 9	106, 433

Table 9-2 DOS/Windows A+ objectives

Objective	Chapters	Page Numbers
Differentiate between types of memory. Content may include the following:		
Conventional	9	439, 440
Extended/upper memory	9	439, 441
High memory	9	439, 445
Expanded memory	9	439, 442, 447
Virtual memory	9	439, 444

REVIEW QUESTIONS

Circle True or False.

1. When you install memory into a PC, the memory must always be installed in pairs. True / False.

2. Conventional memory includes the first 128K of RAM. True / False.

3. EDO stands for extended data output. True / False.

4. EDO RAM is faster than FPM RAM. True / False.

5. Flash memory is commonly used as cache for desktop PCs. True / False.

6. If the following line were added to your CONFIG.SYS file, what would it tell your computer to do?

   DEVICE=C:\DOS\HIMEM.SYS

   _____

   _____

   _____

   _____

   _____

7. What would the following command tell your PC to do?

   EDIT AUTOEXEC.BAT

   _____

   _____

   _____

   _____

   _____

LAB 9.2 MEMORY MANAGEMENT IN DOS AND WINDOWS 3.X

Objective

The objective of this lab exercise is to allow you to familiarize yourself with some common methods of memory management available in the DOS and Windows 3.x environments. After completing this lab exercise, you will be able to:

- Load TSRs from either CONFIG.SYS or AUTOEXEC.BAT.

- Use the MEM command to view your workstation's current memory configuration.

- Create and modify a Windows 3.x swap file.

Materials Required

This lab exercise requires one complete lab workstation for every four students. The lab workstation should meet the following requirements:

- 486 or better
- 8MB of RAM
- Windows 3.x

One disk for each lab workstation containing a TSR.

Lab Setup & Safety Tips

- Each lab workstation should have Windows 3.x installed and functioning properly.

ACTIVITY

Loading a TSR high

1. Allow your lab workstation to boot to DOS.

2. Insert the TSR disk provided by your instructor.

3. Use the COPY command to copy the TSR from the disk to the root directory of your lab workstation.

4. Make the C:\ your current directory.

5. Type **EDIT AUTOEXEC.BAT** and press **Enter**.

6. Add the following to your AUTOEXEC.BAT file (note that the TSR.TSR should be replaced with the name of the TSR on the disk), **LH C:\TSR.TSR**.

7. Press the **Alt** key.

8. Use the down arrow [↓] to select **Save** from the File menu.

9. Press the **Alt** key.

10. Use the down arrow [↓] to select **Exit** from the File menu.

11. Reboot your lab workstation.

12. Verify that the TSR loaded by attempting to use its function.

Using the MEM command

Using the MEM command, fill in the following table:

Memory Type	Total	Used	Free
Conventional memory			
Upper memory			
Reserved memory			
Extended memory			
Totals			
Total memory below 1MB			

Configuring the swap file in the Windows 3.x environment

1. Allow your lab workstation to boot into Windows 3.1.

2. Double-click the **Main** group icon.

3. Double-click **Control Panel**.

4. Double-click the **EMM386** icon.

5. Click the **Virtual Memory** button.

6. Click the **Change** button.

7. Use the drop down arrow to change your swap file settings from Temporary to **Permanent**.

8. Click **OK**.

9. Click the **Restart Windows** button.

Lab Notes

What is a TSR? – A TSR is any program or device driver that resides in memory even though it is not active. Note that TSR stands for terminate and stay resident.

What is HIMEM.SYS? – HIMEM.SYS is a device driver used in the DOS and Windows 3.x environments to manage expanded memory. Note that if HIMEM.SYS fails to load, reboot the PC and check your CONFIG.SYS to verify that the path is specified correctly.

How do I manage a corrupt swap file in Windows 3.x? – A corrupt swap file can be easily managed by booting into DOS, locating the swap file, and then deleting it. Restart the PC and allow it to boot into Windows 3.x. Use the EMM386 icon in the Control Panel to create a new swap file.

A device referenced in the Win.ini could not be found – If you are receiving this error message, run the SYSEDIT utility and verify that all of your recently loaded drivers and files are using the correct path statements.

CERTIFICATION OBJECTIVES

Table 9-3   DOS/Windows A+ objectives

Objective	Chapters	Page Numbers
2.2 Identify typical memory conflict problems and how to optimize memory use. Content may include the following:		
Himem.sys	9	445
4.1 Recognize and interpret the meaning of common error codes, startup messages, and icons from the boot sequence for DOS, Windows 3.x, and Windows 95. Content may include the following:		
Windows 3.x:		
Himem.sys not loaded	9	445
Unable to initialize display adapter	App. E, 2	62, 75, E7
Swapfile corrupt	9	457
A device referenced in Win.ini could not be found	11	521-524

REVIEW QUESTIONS

Circle True or False.

1. TSR stands for terminate safety return. True / False

2. TSRs are programs that stay in memory even when they are not being used. True / False

3. TSRs can only be loaded into memory through the CONFIG.SYS. True / False

4. The MEM command can be used to view the amount of hard drive space available. True / False

5. The HIMEM.SYS file is used to test conventional memory. True / False

6. Which icon on Control Panel is used to modify the Window 3.x memory settings?

_____

_____

_____

_____

_____

7. Describe how to manage a corrupt swap file in Windows 3.x.

_____

_____

_____

_____

_____

LAB 9.3 MEMORY MANAGEMENT IN WINDOWS 95

Objective

The objective of this lab exercise is to teach you how to manage and control memory allocation in the Windows 95 environment. After completing this lab exercise, you will be able to:

- Configure the Windows 95 swap file.

- Edit the Windows 95 CONFIG.SYS and AUTOEXEC.BAT.

- Describe the advantages and disadvantages of using a swap file in Windows 95.

Materials Required

This lab exercise requires one complete lab workstation for every four students. The lab workstation should meet the following requirements:

- 486 or better
- 8MB of RAM
- Windows 95

Lab Setup & Safety Tips

- Each lab workstation should have Windows 95 installed and functioning properly

ACTIVITY

Disabling the Windows 95 swap file

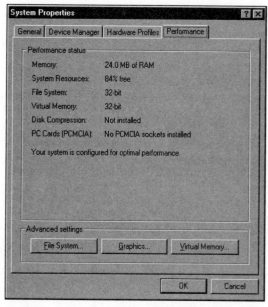

Figure 9-1   System Properties box in Windows 95

1. Allow your lab workstation to boot into Windows 95.

2. Right-click the **My Computer** icon.

3. Select **Properties** from the menu.

4. Click the **Performance** tab.

5. Click the **Virtual Memory** button.

6. Click the **Let me specify my own virtual memory setting** option button.

7. Place a check mark in the **Disable virtual memory** check box.

8. Click the **Yes** button on the confirmation message.

9. Click the **Close** button.

10. Click **Yes** when you are prompted to restart your computer.

11. Observe and describe the results.

_____

_____

_____

_____

_____

Specifying a permanent swap file

1. Allow your lab workstation to boot into Windows 95.

2. Right-click the **My Computer** icon.

3. Select **Properties** from the menu.

4. Click the **Performance** tab.

5. Click the **Virtual Memory** button.

6. Click the **Let me specify my own virtual memory setting** option button.

7. Clear the check mark from the **Disable virtual memory** check box.

8. Set the minimum swap file size to **150MB**.

9. Set the maximum swap file size to **150MB**.

10. Click **OK**.

11. Click the **Yes** button on the confirmation message.

12. Click **Yes** when you are prompted to restart your computer.

13. Observe and describe the results.

_____

_____

_____

_____

_____

Allowing Windows to manage its virtual memory

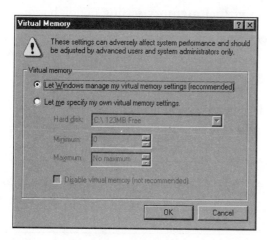

Figure 9-2   Options for managing virtual memory
in Windows 95

1. Allow your lab workstation to boot into Windows 95.

2. Right-click the **My Computer** icon.

3. Select **Properties** from the menu.

4. Click the **Performance** tab.

5. Click the **Virtual Memory** button.

6. Click the **Let Windows manage my virtual memory settings** option button.

7. Click the **OK** button on the confirmation message.

8. Click the **Yes** button on the confirmation message.

9. Click the **Close** button.

10. Click **Yes** when you are prompted to restart your computer.

11. Observe and describe the results.

_____

_____

_____

_____

Lab Notes

What is Windows doing when it manages my virtual memory? – By default, Windows 95 will manage your virtual memory. This means that it will size and resize your swap file as it sees fit. In most circumstances this is the recommended memory management method.

What is a memory conflict, and how does it occur? – A memory conflict occurs when two or more applications attempt to use the same memory address or address range.

What is an illegal operation? – These errors vary depending on the situation. You can find out exactly which applications were involved by clicking the Details button. Many times these errors are GPFs and should be handled accordingly.

CERTIFICATION OBJECTIVES

Table 9-4   DOS/Windows A+ objectives

Objective	Chapters	Page Numbers
2.2 Identify typical memory conflict problems and how to optimize memory use. Content may include the following:		
What a memory conflict is	9	465, 467
How it happens	9	467
Illegal operations occurrences	11	541
Conflicts with 16-bit applications/Windows 95 operations	11	533, 546

REVIEW QUESTIONS

Circle True or False.

1. Windows 95 has the ability to manage its own swap file. True / False

2. It is always recommended that you disable your virtual memory because it isn't needed on new computers. True / False

3. Changing the virtual memory setting in Windows 95 has the same effect as changing the swap file size in Windows 3.x. True / False

4. In Windows 95 each program has its own swap file. True / False

5. How many swap files can Windows 95 use at the same time?

_____

_____

_____

_____

_____

6. You are employed as a desktop PC support technician at the Sweet Town Hot water company. Billy, one of your customers, has asked that you show him how to disable his swap file setting on his laptop. Below, write the instruction for Billy to modify the memory configuration of his laptop.

_____

_____

_____

_____

_____

9

LAB 9.4 MEMORY MANAGEMENT IN WINDOWS NT

Objective

The objective of this lab exercise is to teach you how to manage and control memory allocations in the Windows NT environment. After completing this lab exercise, you will be able to:

- Properly configure one or multiple Windows NT swap files.

- Describe the optimum virtual memory configuration for the Windows NT operating system.

- Configure the maximum registry size.

Materials Required

This lab exercise requires one complete lab workstation for every four students. The lab workstation should meet the following requirements:

- 486 or better
- 16MB of RAM
- Windows NT

Lab Setup & Safety Tips

- Each lab workstation should have Windows NT Workstation installed and functioning properly.

- Each lab workstation must be configured with a D partition.

ACTIVITY

Configuring the Windows NT Swap File

1. Right-click the **My Computer** icon.

2. Click the **Performance** tab.

3. Click the **Change** button.

4. Click in the **Initial Size** box and set the value to **85**.

5. Click in the **Maximum Size** box and set the value to **100**.

6. Click the **Set** button.

7. Click the **OK** button.

8. Click the **Close** button.

9. Click the **Yes** button to restart your lab workstation.

Configuring Multiple Swap Files

1. Right-click the **My Computer** icon.

2. Click the **Performance** tab.

3. Click the **Change** button.

4. At the top of the Virtual Memory property sheet, select drive **D**.

5. Click in the **Initial Size** box and set the value to **85**.

6. Click in the **Maximum Size** box and set the value to **100**.

7. Click the **Set** button.

8. Click the **OK** button.

9. Click the **Close** button.

10. Click the **Yes** button to restart your lab workstation.

Controlling the Windows NT registry size

1. Right-click the **My Computer** icon.

2. Click the **Performance** tab.

3. Click the **Change** button.

4. Click in the **Maximum Registry Size** box and set the value to **10.**

5. Click the **OK** button.

6. Click the **Close** button.

7. Click the **Yes** button to restart your lab workstation.

Lab Notes

What are the ideal virtual memory settings for Windows NT? – To obtain optimum performance from the Windows NT operating system, Microsoft recommends that you place one swap file on each physical hard drive except for the hard drive containing the Windows NT system directory.

What is the ideal registry size? – For most Windows NT installations it isn't necessary to modify the registry size parameter. Should it become necessary to adjust the maximum registry size parameter on a Windows NT Workstation, don't allow it to grow larger than 14MB.

REVIEW QUESTIONS

Circle True or False.

1. Windows NT supports the use of multiple swap files at the same time. True / False

2. When working in the Windows NT environment, it is recommended that you maintain a 20MB swap file at all times. True / False

3. The largest swap file Windows NT workstation supports is 40MB. True / False

4. In Windows NT you have the ability to control the maximum size of the registry. True / False

5. Describe how to configure Windows NT Workstation to use multiple swap files.

_____

_____

_____

_____

_____

6. Jimmy just installed Windows NT workstation on his PC. He has asked you to explain to him how he can move his swap file from his drive C to his drive D. Write the instructions you would give to Jimmy.

_____

_____

_____

_____

_____

ELECTRICITY AND POWER SUPPLIES

LABS INCLUDED IN THIS CHAPTER

LAB **10.1** AC ELECTRICITY

LAB **10.2** DC ELECTRICITY

LAB **10.3** POWER PROTECTION

LAB **10.4** POWER CHAIN TROUBLESHOOTING

LAB 10.1 AC ELECTRICITY

Objective

The objective of this lab exercise is to demonstrate and define some of basic concepts and terminology related to the study and use of electricity. After completing this lab exercise, you will be able to:

- Create a simple switched circuit.
- Describe the relationship between voltage, amperage, ohms and wattage.
- Use a multimeter to measure voltage and amperage.

Materials Required

For this lab exercise each group of four students will require the following materials:

- One 9 volt battery (AA is an acceptable substitute)
- One multimeter (capable of measuring amps)
- One DC light bulb
- One switch
- Three pieces of standard grade electrical wire
- Electrical tape to attach wires to the battery, if necessary

Lab Setup & Safety Tips

- Each group will require a clean desktop area for building their switched circuit.
- The instructor will need to teach the students how to configure the multimeter to measure volts and amps.

ACTIVITY

Creating a circuit

1. Attach one piece of wire to each lead on the light bulb.

2. Attach one of the wires to the batteries lead.

3. Attach the second wire to the other battery lead.

4. Observe the results.

5. In the space provided below, draw a diagram demonstrating the flow of electricity in the circuit you have created. Be sure to note the direction of the current's flow.

Adding a switch

1. Disconnect the wire from the negative side of the battery.

2. Attach the wire to an available lead on the switch.

3. Attach the third wire to the other switch lead and then to the battery.

4. Observe how the switch manages the circuit.

Measuring voltage

1. Configure your multimeter to measure the voltage of your circuit.

2. Attach the +/– leads from your multimeter to the respective +/– sides of the light bulb.

3. Be sure that the switch is turned to the ON position.

4. Record the voltage of your circuit: _____

Measuring amps

1. Configure your multimeter to measure the amps of your circuit.

2. Disconnect the wire that is not currently attached to the switch.

3. Attach the respective +/– side of the multimeter to the battery lead that is not attached to any wires.

4. Attach the respective +/– side of the multimeter to the light bulb that is not attached to any wires.

5. Turn the switch to the ON position.

6. Record the amps found in your circuit: _____

Lab Notes

What does AC mean? – Alternating current (AC) is current that cycles back and forth rather than traveling in only one direction. Normally between 110 and 115 AC volts are supplied from a standard wall outlet.

What are amps? – Amps are a unit of measurement for electrical current. One volt across a resistance of one ohm will produce a flow of one amp.

What are volts? – A volt is a measure of electrical pressure differential. A computer power supply usually provides four separate voltages: +12 V, –12 V, +5 V and –5 V.

What is wattage? – Wattage is a measure of the total amount of power that is needed to operate an electrical device.

What are ohms? – An ohm is the standard unit of measurement for electrical resistance. Resistors are rated in ohms.

REVIEW QUESTIONS

Circle True or False.

1. Resistance is measured in ohms. True / False

2. A switch can act as a break in a circuit. True / False

3. AC is another acronym for ampere. True / False

4. A multimeter can only be used to measure voltage. True / False

5. In a circuit, amps and volts always measure to be the same amount. True / False

6. Describe the difference in multimeter placement for measuring volts and amps.

_____

_____

_____

_____

_____

LAB 10.2 DC ELECTRICITY

Objective

The objective of this lab exercise is to familiarize you with the different functions of a PC's power supply. After completing this lab exercise, you will be able to:

- Describe the function of a PC power supply.

- Use a multimeter to test and measure PC power supplies output.

- Successfully troubleshoot power supply issues.

Materials Required

This lab exercise requires one complete lab workstation for every four students. The lab workstation should meet the following requirements:

- 486 or better
- 8MB of RAM
- Windows 95

One multimeter

Tools necessary to remove the lab workstation's case and power supply

Lab Setup & Safety Tips

- Each lab workstation should be in good working order.

- Students should always follow proper ESD procedures when working with computer components.

- For the purpose of this lab exercise the systemboard power connectors will be referred to as the P8 and P9 connectors.

- If students are working in pairs, assign Student 1 and Student 2.

ACTIVITY

Measuring the +12VDC wire of a PC's power supply

1. Unplug your lab workstation.

2. Configure your multimeter to measure voltages within the following range –5 V DC/+15 V DC.

3. Remove the case.

4. Using Figure 10-1 for reference, attach the respective multimeter leads to the ground and +12 V wires (connect the multimeter to the power supply connector outside of the case on a flat surface that can be easily seen and controlled).

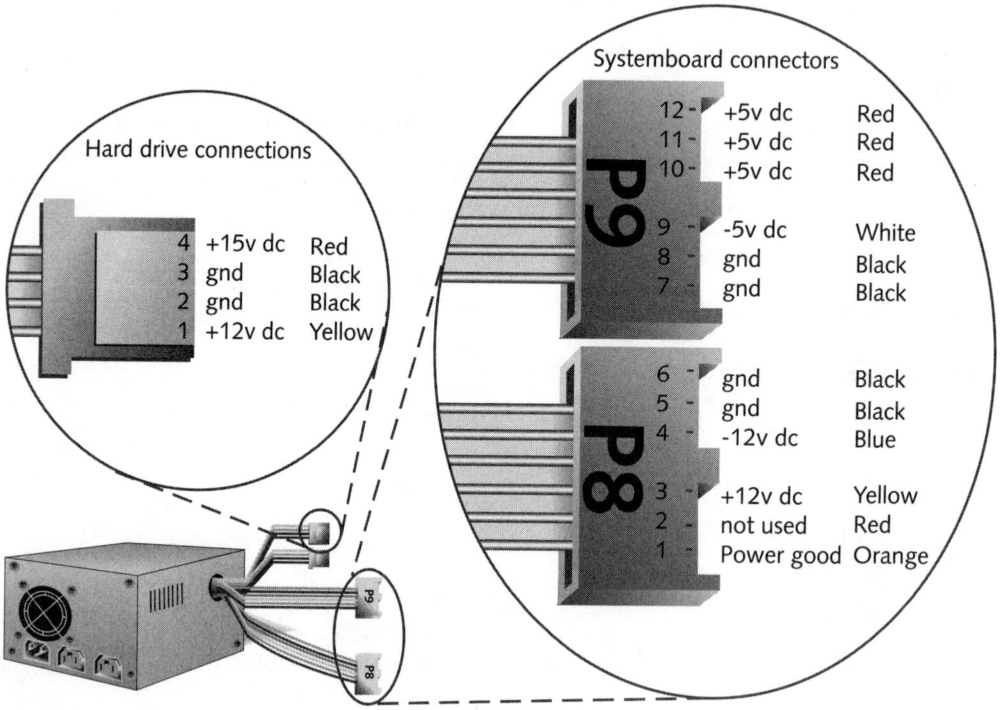

Figure 10-1   Power supply connections

5. Before plugging in the PC, verify that no other metal pieces are touching the system-board or power supply, which could cause a short.

6. Plug in the power cord.

7. Stand clear of the lab workstation and power it on.

8. Record the results displayed on the multimeter: _____

9. Refer to the table below to verify that the recorded voltage falls within the acceptable range.

10. Power off your lab workstation.

Table 10-1   Twelve leads to the systemboard from the power supply

Connection	Lead	Description	Acceptable Range
P8	1	"Power Good"	
	2	Not used	
	3	+12 volts	+8.5 to +12.6 volts
	4	–12 volts	–8.5 to –12.6 volts
	5	Black ground	
	6	Black ground	
P9	7	Black ground	
	8	Black ground	
	9	–5 volts	–4.5 to –5.4 volts
	10	+5 volts	+2.4 to +5.2 volts
	11	+5 volts	+2.4 to +5.2 volts
	12	+5 volts	+2.4 to +5.2 volts

Measuring the +15 V DC wire of a PC's power supply

1. Unplug your lab workstation.

2. Configure your multimeter to measure voltages within the following range: −5 V DC/+15 V DC.

3. Using Figure 10-1, attach the respective multimeter leads to the ground and +15 V DC wires (connect the multimeter to the power supply connector outside of the case on a flat surface that can be easily seen and controlled).

4. Before plugging in the PC, verify that no other metal pieces are touching the systemboard or power supply, which could cause a short.

5. Plug in the power cord.

6. Stand clear of the lab workstation and power it on.

7. Record the results displayed on the multimeter: _____

8. Refer to the table from the previous activity to verify that the recorded voltage falls within the acceptable range.

9. Power off your lab workstation.

Measuring the +5 V DC wire of the P9 systemboard power connector

1. Unplug your lab workstation.

2. Configure your multimeter to measure voltages within the following range −5 V DC/+15 V DC.

3. Using Figure 10-1, attach the respective multimeter leads to the ground and +5 V DC wires (connect the multimeter to the power supply connector outside of the case on a flat surface that can be easily seen and controlled).

4. Before plugging in the PC, verify that no other metal pieces or objects are touching the systemboard or power supply, which could cause a short.

5. Plug in the power cord.

6. Stand clear of the lab workstation and power it on.

7. Record the results displayed on the multimeter: _____

8. Refer to the table from the first exercise to verify that the recorded voltage falls within the acceptable range.

Measuring the +12 V DC wire of the P8 systemboard power connector

1. Unplug your lab workstation.

2. Configure your multimeter to measure voltages within the following range −5 V DC/+15 V DC

3. Using Figure 10-1, attach the respective multimeter leads to the ground and +12 V DC wires (connect the multimeter to the power supply connector outside of the case on a flat surface that can be easily seen and controlled)

4. Before plugging in the PC, verify that no other metal pieces or objects are touching the systemboard or power supply, which could cause a short.

5. Plug in the power cord.

6. Stand clear of the lab workstation and power it on.

7. Record the results displayed on the multimeter: _____

8. Refer to the table from the first exercise to verify that the recorded voltage falls within the acceptable range.

10

Removing a power supply

Student 1

1. Unplug your lab workstation.

2. Unplug all of the power connectors.

3. Locate the mounting screws of the power supply.

4. Unscrew and dismount the power supply.

5. Hand the power supply and mounting screws to Student 2.

Installing a power supply

Student 2

1. Place the power supply into the mounting position.

2. After verifying that the power supply is properly aligned, screw the screws into place.

3. Attach each of the power connectors to their respective devices.

4. Plug in the power cord.

5. Power on the lab workstation and verify that all of the devices are functioning properly.

Lab Notes

Are power connectors for SCSI devices different from those for IDE devices? – No, the power connectors generally used for SCSI devices provide the same functionality as they would for an IDE device.

CERTIFICATION OBJECTIVES

Table 10-2   Core A+ objectives

Objective	Chapters	Page Numbers
1.1 Identify basic terms, concepts, and functions of system modules, including how each module should work during normal operation. Examples of concepts and modules:		
Power supply	1, 3	10, 37, 124
1.2 Identify basic procedures for adding and removing field replaceable modules. Examples of modules:		
Power supply	10	498-500
1.6 Identify proper procedures for installing and configuring SCSI devices. Content may include the following:		
Power supply	10	497
1.8 Recognize the functions and effective use of common hand tools. Content may include the following:		
Torx bit	7	337
Regular bit	7	337
Multimeter	7	337, 491-497
2.1 Identify common symptoms and problems associated with each module and how to troubleshoot and isolate the problems. Content may include the following:		
Power supply	App. E	E15

Table 10-2   Core A+ objectives (continued)

Objective	Chapters	Page Numbers
3.2 Identify procedures and devices for protecting against environmental hazards. Content may include the Following:		
Determining the signs of power issues	10	490, 498
3.3 Identify the potential hazards and proper safety procedures relating to lasers and high voltage equipment.		
High voltage equipment can cause electrocution, e.g.,	7	334
Power supply	Introduction	xxiii

REVIEW QUESTIONS

Circle True or False.

1. A hard drive connector's red wire should have a voltage that falls within the range of −15 V DC to +15 V DC. True / False

2. The P8 and P9 connectors are designed to be used for SCSI devices. True / False

3. Removing a power supply is as simple as removing the power connectors and dismounting the power supply. True / False

4. There should always be at least one ground wire per power connector. True / False

5. The ground wire should have a voltage reading that falls within the ranges of −5 V DC to −15 V DC. True / False

6. The power supply is normally mounted to the systemboard. True / False

7. Ginger's PC keeps rebooting by itself. She suspects that the power supply is faulty. Describe below why or why not Ginger's suspicion is a realistic possibility.

   _____

   _____

   _____

   _____

   _____

8. John tested one of his power supply connectors by attaching his multimeter's leads to the two center wires of a hard drive connector with the system powered on. He received a reading of 0 volts. He now believes that he will need to replace the power supply. Describe below why or why not John should replace the power supply.

   _____

   _____

   _____

   _____

   _____

10

LAB 10.3 POWER PROTECTION

Objective

The objective of this lab exercise is to allow you install and configure a surge protector and an uninterruptible power supply (UPS) device. After completing this lab exercise, you will be able to:

- Describe the functionality of a surge protector.
- Properly install and configure a surge protector.
- Describe the functionality of a UPS device.
- Properly install and configure a UPS device.
- Properly install and configure a power conditioner.

Materials Required

This lab exercise requires one complete lab workstation for every four students. The lab workstations should meet the following requirements:

- 486 or better
- 4MB of RAM
- Windows 95

One surge protector

One UPS device of any type

One power conditioner

Lab Setup & Safety Tips

- Each lab workstation should have Windows 95 installed and functioning properly.
- Students should always follow proper ESD procedures when working with computer components.

ACTIVITY

Installing a surge protector

1. Power off your lab workstation.
2. Power off your monitor and any other peripheral devices.
3. Plug the provided surge protector into the wall outlet.
4. Plug each of your peripheral devices into the surge protector (this includes the system unit and monitor).
5. Power on the surge protector.
6. Power on your lab workstation.
7. Power on your monitor and other peripheral devices (this includes the system unit and monitor).
8. Verify that your PC is functioning properly.

Installing a UPS device

1. Power off your system unit.

2. Power off any additional peripherals you want to be protected by the UPS device.

3. Unplug the system unit and the peripheral devices.

4. Plug the UPS device into the wall outlet.

5. Plug the system unit into the UPS device.

6. Plug the additionally protected devices into the UPS.

7. Power on the UPS device.

8. Power on the system unit and additionally protected peripherals.

9. Verify that the system unit and each additionally protected device is functioning properly.

Observing the functionality of a UPS device

1. Power on your system unit and allow it to boot into Windows 95.

2. Power on your additionally protected devices.

3. Unplug the UPS device.

4. Record the results.

_____

_____

_____

Installing a power conditioner

1. Power off your system unit.

2. Power off any additional peripherals you want to be protected by the power conditioner.

3. Unplug the system unit and the peripheral devices.

4. Plug the provided power conditioner into the wall outlet.

5. Plug the system unit into the power conditioner.

6. Plug the additionally protected devices into the power conditioner.

7. Power on the system unit and additionally protected peripherals.

8. Verify that the system unit and each additionally protected device is functioning properly.

Lab Notes

What is an in-line UPS? – An in-line UPS is a device that continually provides power through a battery-powered circuit and because it requires no switching, it ensures continuous power to the user.

What is a standby UPS? – A standby UPS is a device that quickly switches from an AC power source to a battery-powered source during a brownout or outage.

What is an intelligent UPS? – An intelligent UPS is connected to a computer by way of a serial cable so that software on the computer can monitor and control the UPS.

What is a power conditioner? – A power conditioner is a device that regulates, or conditions, the power, providing continuous voltage during brownouts.

CERTIFICATION OBJECTIVES

Table 10-3   Core A+ objectives

Objective	Chapters	Page Numbers
3.2 Identify procedures and devices for protecting against environmental hazards. Content may include the Following:		
UPS (uninterruptible power supply), suppressors, noise filters, and plug strips	10	508-511
Proper methods of storage of components for future use	6	264, 335, 336

REVIEW QUESTIONS

Circle True or False.

1. All UPS devices provide the same functionality. True / False

2. A power conditioner will provide battery power for five minutes in the case of an outage. True / False

3. Surge protectors eventually deteriorate. True / False

4. An intelligent UPS can be controlled by software. True / False

5. Describe how a surge protector provides protection from power spikes.

_____

_____

_____

_____

_____

6. You are employed as a network administrator at Pictures Inc. Your employer has asked you to assess the need for UPS devices for each of their 10 servers. After talking with the staff you discover that 7 of the servers are used for email and bulletin board communications. The other 3 servers are used to maintain all of the company's accounting inventory databases. Pictures, Inc. has asked that you provide two proposals for them, the first outlining the ideal protection plan, and the other outlining the minimum protection requirements.

Power Protection Plan A (ideal)

_____

_____

_____

_____

Power Protection Plan B (cost-effective)

_____

_____

_____

_____

_____

LAB 10.4 POWER CHAIN TROUBLESHOOTING

Objective

The objective of this lab exercise is to allow you the opportunity to develop your electrical troubleshooting skills. After completing this lab exercise, you will be able to:

- Identify a power issue.
- Repair an electrical problem.
- Describe some common symptoms of electrical problems.

Materials Required

This lab exercise requires one complete lab workstation for every four students. The lab workstations should meet the following requirements:

- 486 or better
- 4MB of RAM
- Windows 95

Tools necessary to remove the lab workstation's case.

Lab Setup & Safety Tips

- Each lab workstation should have Windows 95 installed and functioning properly.
- Students should always follow proper ESD procedures when working with computer components.
- If students are working in pairs, assign Student 1 and Student 2.

ACTIVITY

Troubleshooting a power supply

Student 1

The following should be completed while Student 2 is away from the lab workstation:

1. Power off your lab workstation.
2. Unplug the power cord.
3. Remove the case.
4. Unplug the P8 connector from the systemboard.
5. Replace the case.
6. Plug in the power cord.
7. Power on the lab workstation.

Student 2

After Student 1 has reconfigured the lab workstation, answer the following questions, and then repair the lab workstation:

1. Are there any error messages? If so, write them down:

_____

_____

10

2. What is the problem (be specific)? _____

3. List several possible solutions: _____

4. Test your theory (solution) and record the results:

_____

_____

5. How did you discover the problem?

_____

_____

_____

6. What could you do differently next time to improve your troubleshooting process?

_____

_____

_____

_____

_____

_____

Student 2

The following should be completed while Student 1 is away from the lab workstation:

1. Power off your lab workstation.

2. Unplug the power cord.

3. Remove the case.

4. Reverse to P8 and P9 power connectors.

5. Replace the case.

6. Plug in the power cord.

7. Power on the lab workstation.

Student 1

After Student 2 has reconfigured the lab workstation, answer the following questions and repair the lab workstation:

1. Are there any error messages? If so, write them down:

_____

_____

2. What is the problem (be specific)? _____

3. List several possible solutions: _____

4. Test your theory (solution) and record the results:

_____

_____

5. How did you discover the problem?

_____

_____

_____

6. What could you do differently next time to improve your troubleshooting process?

_____

_____

_____

_____

_____

_____

Lab Notes

How should I repair a power supply that is shorting? – As a PC technician you should never open or attempt to repair the internal working of a power supply. A PC technician's job should is to diagnose the problem and if necessary replace the power supply.

An electrical troubleshooting tip – When troubleshooting electricity, mentally follow the path the electricity follows, starting from the wall outlet and working its way through the entire PC. In this way it will quickly become obvious which part of a PC is having a power problem and more importantly, which device is causing the electrical problem.

CERTIFICATION OBJECTIVES

Table 10-4   Core A+ objectives

Objective	Chapters	Page Numbers
1.1 Identify basic terms, concepts, and functions of system modules, including how each module should work during normal operation. Examples of concepts and modules:		
Power supply	1, 3	10, 37, 124
1.8 Recognize the functions and effective use of common hand tools. Content may include the following:		
Regular bit	7	337

REVIEW QUESTIONS

Circle True or False.

1. If a power supply's fan does not spin, it could indicate that the power supply has failed.
True / False

2. The P8 and P9 power connectors can be attached to the systemboard in any order.
True / False

3. Hard drive connectors and the systemboard connector use the same voltage. True / False

4. A common mistake is to attach the hard drive power connector to the systemboard.
True / False

5. What should the voltage of a power supply's ground wires be?

_____

_____

_____

_____

_____

6. Elliot has just replaced his systemboard, but now his computer won't boot. List three possible power-related problems that could be wrong with his system.

_____

_____

_____

_____

_____

CHAPTER ELEVEN

SUPPORTING WINDOWS 3.X AND WINDOWS 95

LABS INCLUDED IN THIS CHAPTER

LAB 11.1 INSTALLING WINDOWS 3.X

LAB 11.2 CUSTOMIZING WINDOWS 3.X

LAB 11.3 INSTALLING WINDOWS 95

LAB 11.4 CUSTOMIZING WINDOWS 95

LAB 11.1 INSTALLING WINDOWS 3.X

Objective

The objective of this lab exercise is to allow you to install Windows 3.x. After completing this lab exercise, you will be able to:

- Install Windows 3.x.
- Describe the Windows 3.x installation process.
- Locate and describe the function of Windows 3.x system files.

Materials Required

This lab exercise requires one complete lab workstation for every four students. The lab workstation should meet the following requirements:

- 486 or better
- 4MB of RAM
- Window 3.x installation files

One DOS system disk

Lab Setup & Safety Tips

- Each lab workstation should be preloaded with the Windows 3.x installation files, which should be placed in a directory named C:\WIN3.1.

ACTIVITY

Installing Windows 3.1

1. Insert the system disk into drive A.

2. Power on your lab workstation and allow it to boot from the DOS system disk.

3. At the C prompt, type **CD C:\WIN3.1** and press **Enter**.

4. Type **SETUP** and press **Enter**. Your lab workstation should respond by beginning the Windows 3.x installation.

5. Press **Enter**.

6. Press **Enter** to select the Express Setup option.

7. Press the **Backspace** key to clear the Windows system directory path.

8. Type **C:\WINDOWS3.1** and press **Enter**.

9. Type your name and press **Enter**.

10. Press **Enter**.

11. Click the **Cancel** button to skip the printer driver installation.

12. Click the **Skip** button.

13. Click the **Reboot** button.

Identifying Windows 3.x system files

1. Using your lab workstation and textbook for reference, write the path of the following system files and describe their functionality.

   a. WIN.INI _____

   _____

   _____

   _____

   b. SYSTEM.INI _____

   _____

   _____

   _____

   c. USER.EXE _____

   _____

   _____

   _____

   d. GDI.EXE _____

   _____

   _____

   _____

   e. WIN.COM _____

   _____

   _____

   _____

Lab Notes

Express Setup – Express Setup allows Windows 3.x to automatically install a group of preselected operating system components.

Custom Setup – Custom Setup allows you to select the components that you want to install.

Reinstalling Windows – This option, sometimes referred to as upgrading Windows, allows you to install Windows 3.x over the currently installed version. You can use this option to repair a damaged installation of Windows 3.x.

What do I do if the setup program stops? – If the setup program stops, it is most likely having problems detecting one or more of your hardware devices. To skip the detection process, reboot the PC and restart the setup program using the following command: C:\WIN3.1\SETUP /I.

CERTIFICATION OBJECTIVES

Table 11-1   DOS/Windows A+ objectives

Objective	Chapters	Page Numbers
1.1 Identify the operating system's functions, structure, and major system files. Content may include the following:		
Functions of DOS, Windows 3.x and Windows 95	1	20-22
Major components of DOS, Windows 3.x and Windows 95	1, 11, 12	20-22, 547, 604-606
Contrasts between Windows 3.x and Windows 95	1	20-22
Major system files: what they are, where they are located and how they are used:	11	521, 524, 537, 545
System, Configuration, and User Interface files	12	628
Windows 3.x:		
Win.ini	2, 11	68, 521, 522
System.ini	2, 11	68, 521
User.exe	11	547
Gdi.exe	11	546-547
Win.com	11	521
3.1 Identify the procedures for installing DOS, Windows 3.x, and Windows 95, and bringing the software to a basic operational level. Content may include the following:		
Run appropriate setup utility	11	527, 551

REVIEW QUESTIONS

Circle True or False.

1. To install Windows 3.x you must run the install program. True / False

2. The WIN.INI stores the setting for the Windows 3.x swap file. True / False

3. Choosing the Custom Setup option during the Windows 3.x installation process will allow you to choose the Windows 3.x components you want to have installed. True / False

4. Windows 3.x must always be installed in a directory named Windows. True / False

5. The SYSTEM.INI stores Windows 3.x application configuration data. True / False

6. Lily wants to install Windows 3.x on her laptop. She has copied the installation files to her hard drive and run the setup program. The Windows setup program is now asking her whether she wants to use the Express Setup or Custom Setup. She has asked you to describe the difference to her; she doesn't want to make a mistake. Write your answer to Lily below:

_____

_____

_____

_____

LAB 11.2 CUSTOMIZING WINDOWS 3.X

Objective

This lab exercise is designed to allow you the opportunity to configure some of the more commonly used settings in the Windows 3.x environment. After completing this lab exercise, you will be able to:

- Properly configure Windows 3.x to use a screen saver, desktop wallpaper, and customized groups.

- Describe how the Startup group is used in the Windows 3.x environment.

Materials Required

This lab exercise requires one complete lab workstation for every four students. The lab workstations should meet the following requirements:

- 486 or better
- 4MB of RAM
- Windows 3.x

Lab Setup & Safety Tips

- Each lab workstation should have Windows 3.x installed and functioning properly.

ACTIVITY

Configuring your desktop wallpaper in the Windows 3.x environment

1. Power on your lab workstation and allow it to boot into Windows 3.x.

2. Open the Program Manager window.

3. Double-click the **Main** group icon.

4. Double-click the **Control Panel** icon.

5. Double-click the **Desktop** icon.

6. Locate the Wallpaper heading.

7. Click the drop-down arrow under the Wallpaper heading.

8. Select the **zigzag.bmp** option.

9. Click the **OK** button. Your lab workstation should respond by displaying a zigzag pattern behind the Program Manager window.

Configuring your screen saver in the Windows 3.x environment

1. Power on your lab workstation and allow it to boot into Windows 3.x.

2. Open the **Program Manager** window.

3. Double-click the **Main** group icon.

4. Double-click the **Control Panel** icon.

5. Double-click the **Desktop** icon.

6. Locate the Screen Saver heading.

7. Click the drop-down arrow under the Screen Saver heading.

8. Select the **Mystify** option.

9. Click the **OK** button. Your lab workstation should respond by displaying the Mystify screen saver after the screen saver time period has expired.

Creating a personalized program group

1. Power on your lab workstation and allow it to boot into Windows 3.x.

2. Open the Program Manager window.

3. Click the **File** menu.

4. Select **New**.

5. Click the **Program Group** option button.

6. Click the **OK** button.

7. Type **MY GROUP** in the Description box.

8. Type **MY GROUP** in the Group File box.

9. Click the **OK** button.

10. Locate your new group in the Program Manager window, and then double-click it.

Using the Startup group

The Startup group is used to configure your operating system to automatically start a program or programs when the operating system has completed initialization. To start a program automatically, execute the following steps:

1. Power on your lab workstation and allow it to boot into Windows 3.x.

2. Open the Program Manager window.

3. Double-click the **Startup** group icon.

4. Double-click the **Accessories** group icon.

5. Drag the **Notepad** icon from the **Accessories** group to the **Startup** group.

6. Close the Startup group and the Accessories group.

7. Click the **File** menu in the Program Manager window.

8. Select **Exit Windows**.

9. Click **OK** in the confirmation message box.

10. At the C prompt, type **WIN**.

11. When windows has restarted, notice that the Notepad program is executed after the operating system has been initialized.

Lab Notes

DOS commands and Windows 3.x utilities

MSD – MSD stands for Microsoft System Diagnostics; this utility was originally designed to help you identify and resolve resource conflicts in the DOS environment.

MEM – The MEM command is used to view how memory is being allocated in the DOS environment.

SCANDISK – The SCANDISK utility is designed to check the FAT for cross-linked files and other inconsistences and to repair them if necessary.

DEFRAG – The DEFRAG utility is used to reorganize clusters on your hard drive in order to improve disk performance.

SYSEDIT – This utility is used in the Windows environment. SYSEDIT allows you to view and make changes to all of the most commonly used configuration files, such as the AUTOEXEC.BAT, CONFIG.SYS, WIN.INI, SYSTEM.INI, and so on.

Where can I get more information about Windows 3.x? – You can always purchase a Windows 3.x user's manual, but even easier and more cost-effective is reading the documentation included with the operating system. The following five files are located in the Windows directory:

Readme.wri

Printers.wri

Networks.wri

Sysini.wri

Winini.wri

CERTIFICATION OBJECTIVES

Table 11-2   DOS/Windows A+ objectives

Objective	Chapters	Page Numbers
1.2 Identify ways to navigate the operating system and how to get to needed technical information. Content may include the following:		
Procedures for navigating through the Windows 3.x/Windows 95 operating system, accessing, and retrieving information	5	214-219
4.6 Identify the purpose of and procedures for using various DOS and Windows-based utilities and commands/switches to diagnose and troubleshoot problems. Content may include the following:		
DOS:		
MSD.exe	8	397-398
Windows-based tools:		
Scandisk	4, 5, 7	153, 161, 223-224, 338
Defrag.exe	5, 6, 7	221-222, 251, 290, 312, 338
Conflict troubleshooter	9	466
Sysedit.exe	11	522

11

REVIEW QUESTIONS

Circle True or False.

1. You can configure you desktop wallpaper via the Accessories group. True / False

2. The term desktop wallpaper refers to the .BMP file displayed as the background on your computer screen. True / False

3. You cannot create any additional groups in the Program Manager window. True / False

4. You can configure Windows 3.x to automatically start applications. True / False

5. A screen saver can be configured via the Control Panel Desktop icon. True / False

6. Alice wants to create a program group containing all of her most commonly used applications. Describe below how Alice could accomplish this task.

_____

_____

_____

_____

_____

LAB 11.3 INSTALLING WINDOWS 95

Objective

The objective of this lab exercise is for you to install the Windows 95 operating system. After completing this lab exercise, you will be able to:

- Install Windows 95.

- Accurately describe the Windows 95 installation process.

- Locate and describe the function of Windows 95 system files.

Materials Required

This lab exercise requires one complete lab workstation for every four students. The lab workstations should meet the following requirements:

- 486 or better
- 8MB of RAM
- Windows 95 installation files

One DOS system disk

One blank formatted disk

A valid Windows 95 product ID for each lab workstation

Lab Setup & Safety Tips

- Each lab workstation should be preloaded with the Windows 95 installation files, which should be placed in a directory named C:\WIN95.

ACTIVITY

Installing Windows 95

1. Insert the system disk into drive A.

2. Power on your lab workstation and allow it to boot from the DOS system disk.

3. At the C prompt, type **CD C:\WIN95** and press **Enter**.

4. Type **SETUP** and press **Enter**.

5. Press **Enter** to allow the setup program to run the SCANDISK utility.

6. Click the **Continue** button.

7. Click the **Yes** button.

8. Click the **Next** button.

9. Select the **Other Directory** option and click the **Next** button.

10. Type **C:\WINDOWS.95** and click the **Next** button.

11. Type the product ID provided by your instructor.

12. Type your name.

13. Click the **Next** button.

14. Select the hardware components that pertain to your lab workstation, and click the **Next** button.

15. Click the **Next** button.

16. Click the **Next** button.
17. Click the **Next** button.
18. Click the **Next** button.
19. Insert your blank floppy disk into drive A.
20. Click the **OK** button.
21. Remove the floppy disk and click the **OK** button.
22. Click the **Finish** button.
23. Select the proper time zone, and click the **OK** button.
24. Click the **Cancel** button when prompted to install a printer driver.
25. Click the **Restart** button.

Identifying Windows 95 system files

1. Using your lab workstation and textbook for reference, write the path of the following system files and describe their functionality.

a. IO.SYS _____
_____
_____
_____

b. MSDOS.SYS _____
_____
_____
_____

c. COMMAND.COM _____
_____
_____
_____

d. WIN.INI _____
_____
_____
_____

e. PROGMAN.INI _____
_____
_____
_____

f. SYSTEM.DAT _____
_____
_____
_____

g. USER.DAT _____
_____
_____
_____

11

Lab Notes

What do I do if the Setup program stops? – If the Windows 95 Setup program stops during the installation, you can restart it by simply rebooting the PC and running the setup program again. Unlike Windows 3.x however, Windows 95 has the added ability to learn from its mistakes. For example, if Windows 95 crashes during the installation process, when you restart, the program will automatically skip the process that hung the system during the previous installation attempt.

Express Setup – Express Setup allows Windows 95 to automatically install a group of preselected operating system components.

Custom Setup – Custom Setup allows you to select the components that you want to have installed.

Reinstalling Windows – This option, sometimes referred to as upgrading Windows, allows you to install Windows 95 over the currently installed version. You can use this option to repair a damaged installation of Windows 95.

CERTIFICATION OBJECTIVES

Table 11-3   DOS/Windows A+ objectives

Objective	Chapters	Page Numbers
1.1 Identify the operating system's functions, structure, and major system files. Content may include the following:		
Major components of DOS, Windows 3.x and Windows 95	1, 11, 12	20-22, 547, 604-606
Major system files: what they are, where they are located and how they are used:	11	521, 524, 537, 545
System, Configuration, and User Interface files	12	628
Windows 95 :		
Io.sys	2	70, 148, 161
Msdos.sys	11	572
Command.com	2, 4	67, 151, 161
Win.ini	2, 11	68, 521, 522
Progman.ini	2, 11	68, 521, 522
System.dat	11	571, 572
User.dat	11	571, 572
3.1 Identify the procedures for installing DOS, Windows 3.x, and Windows 95, and bringing the software to a basic operational level. Content may include the following:		
Run appropriate set up utility	11	527, 551
Loading drivers	8, 11	389-391, 544
3.2 Identify steps to perform an operating system upgrade. Content may include the following:		
Upgrading from DOS to Win95	11	559
Loading drivers	8, 11	389-391, 544
4.3 Identify the steps to create an emergency boot disk with utilities installed	7	338

REVIEW QUESTIONS

Circle True or False.

1. Windows 3.x and Windows 95 use the exact same setup program. True / False

2. During the Windows 95 installation, you are given the option to install MSN connectivity. True / False

3. The Windows 95 setup program executes the SCANDISK utility before installing or upgrading the operating system. True / False

4. During the Windows 95 installation, you are given an opportunity to create an emergency repair disk. True / False

5. What are the filenames of the SYSTEM.DAT and the USER.DAT backup files created automatically by Windows 95?

   _____

   _____

   _____

   _____

   _____

6. If you were installing Windows 95 on a laptop, which of the following component packages would be ideal, and why or why not?

   - Typical
   - Custom
   - Portable

   _____

   _____

   _____

   _____

   _____

11

LAB 11.4 CUSTOMIZING WINDOWS 95

Objective

This lab exercise is designed to allow you the opportunity to configure some of the more commonly used settings in the Windows 95 environment. After completing this lab exercise, you will be able to:

- Properly configure Windows 95 to use a screen saver, desktop wallpaper, and customized shortcuts.

- Modify the Start menu.

- Install a printer driver in the Windows 95 environment.

Materials Required

This lab exercise requires one complete lab workstation for every four students. The lab workstations should meet the following requirements:

- 486 or better
- 8MB of RAM
- Windows 95

Lab Setup & Safety Tips

- Each lab workstation should have Windows 95 installed and functioning properly.

ACTIVITY

Configuring your desktop wallpaper in Windows 95

1. Power on your lab workstation and allow it to boot into Windows 95.

2. Right-click the desktop.

3. Select **Properties** from the menu.

4. Locate the section with the Wallpaper heading.

5. Scroll down in the Wallpaper box, and click the Clouds wallpaper.

6. Click the **Apply** button.

7. Click the **OK** button.

Configuring your screen saver in Windows 95

1. Power on your lab workstation and allow it to boot into Windows 95.

2. Right-click the desktop.

3. Select **Properties** from the menu.

4. Click the **Screen Saver** tab.

5. Locate the drop-down arrow under the **Screen Saver** heading.

6. Click the drop-down arrow and select the **Mystify** option.

7. Click the **Apply** button.

8. Click the **OK** button.

Creating personalized program shortcuts

1. Right-click the desktop.

2. Select **New** from the menu.

3. Click **Shortcut**.

4. Type **C:\WINDOWS.95\WINFILE.EXE** and press **Enter**.

5. In the Select name of Shortcut box, type **File Manager**.

6. Click the **Finish** button.

Customizing your Start menu

1. Right-click the taskbar.

2. Select **Properties** from the menu.

Figure 11-1   Windows 95 taskbar shortcut menu

3. Click the **Start Menu Programs** tab.

4. Click the **Add** button.

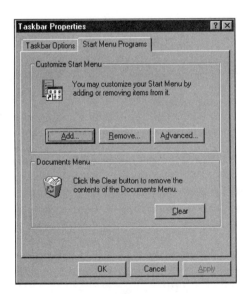

Figure 11-2   Taskbar Properties dialog box

5. Type **C:\WINDOWS\WINFILE.EXE**.

6. Click the **Next** button.

7. Double-click the **Accessories** folder.

8. In the Select name of Shortcut box, type **File Manager**.

9. Click the **Finish** button.

10. Click the **OK** button.

11. Verify that the shortcut was properly added to the Accessories group by clicking the **Start** button, pointing to **Programs**, and then clicking **Accessories**.

12. Click the newly created **File Manager** shortcut.

Installing a printer driver

1. Power on your lab workstation and allow it to boot into Windows 95.

2. Double-click the **My Computer** icon.

3. Double-click the **Printers** folder.

4. Double-click **Add New Printer**.

5. Click the **Next** button.

6. Choose the **My computer** option, and click the **Next** button.

7. Choose the correct printer driver by selecting the appropriate manufacturer and then the printer model. Click the **OK** button when you are done.

8. Select the appropriate printer port, and click the **Next** button.

9. Click the **Next** button again to use the default printer name.

10. Click the **Finish** button to complete the printer driver installatation.

Lab Notes

What is Safe Mode? – Safe Mode is a way of starting Windows 95 with a minimal amount of Windows drivers. Note that Safe Mode is designed to be used for troubleshooting purposes.

What is DOS Mode? – Like Windows 3.x, Windows 95 uses DOS as its underlying operating system. DOS 7.0 is the version used by the Windows 95; therefore DOS mode is simply a DOS 7.0 command prompt.

How can I enable multiboot? – In the Windows 95 environment, you can edit the MSDOS.SYS file to create a multiboot environment.

How do I install applications? – Most Windows application come with a setup program that is designed to automatically install the application after you answer a few simple questions.

Symptoms of a stalled print spooler in Windows 95 – When the Windows 95 print spooler stalls, the operating system will at first appear to hang (stop responding). After the operating system has recovered, you will notice that when accessing the Printer folder, none of your printer icons will appear. The fastest way to resolve a spooler problem in Windows 95 is to simply reboot the PC.

The printer won't print at all. Now what? – When working with printers in any environment, you should always verify the following settings:

- Verify that the printer, CMOS, and operating system are all configured to use the same type of cable (bi-directional, unidirectional, ECP, EPP).

- Verify that the operating system has the correct printer driver installed.

- Check the spooler; be sure it has not stalled.

- Verify that the printer driver is configured to use the proper printer port (LPT1, COM1, LPT2)

Where can I get more information about Windows 95? – You can always purchase a Windows 95 user's manual, but even easier and more cost-effective is using the built-in Help features of Windows 95. You can find the Windows 95 Help by simply clicking the Start button and then clicking Help.

What is the Conflict Troubleshooter? – The Conflict Troubleshooter is an interactive Help menu designed to help you resolve resource conflicts in the Windows 95 environment.

How do I get help? – All Microsoft operating systems are released with integrated Help. To quickly access the Help menu in Windows 95, click anywhere on the desktop or press the F1 key.

CERTIFICATION OBJECTIVES

A+

Table 11-4   DOS/Windows A+ objectives

Objective	Chapters	Page Numbers
1.1 Identify the operating system's functions, structure, and major system files. Content may include the following:		
Functions of DOS, Windows 3.x and Windows 95	1	20-22
Major components of DOS, Windows 3.x and Windows 95	1, 11, 12	20-22, 547, 604-606
Contrasts between Windows 3.x and Windows 95	1	20-22
System, Configuration, and User Interface files	12	628
1.2 Identify ways to navigate the operating system and how to get to needed technical information. Content may include the following:		
Procedures for navigating through the Windows 3.x/Windows 95 operating system, accessing, and retrieving information	5	214-219
3.3 Identify the basic system boot sequences for DOS, Windows 3.x, and Windows 95, and alternative ways to boot the system software. Content may include the following:		
Safe mode	11	561
DOS mode	11	561
Multi-boot configurations	11	559-563
3.6 Identify the procedures for changing options, configuring, and using the Windows printing subsystem	12, 13, App. E	622, 695, E9
3.7 Identify the procedures for installing and launching typical Windows and non-Windows applications.	11, 12	530, 634-636
4.4 Recognize Windows-specific printing problems and identify the procedures for correcting them. Content may include the following:		
Print spool is stalled	16	884
Driver is set for bi-directional printing, but user is using a unidirectional cable	16, App. E	884, E8-E10
Incorrect/incompatible driver for print	12, App. E	622, E8-E10
Printer port is not set up correctly in device manager (ECP, EPP, Standard)	12, App. E	622, E8-E10
Printer not set up to print to Correct port	12, App. E	622, E8-E10
4.6 Identify the purpose of and procedures for using various DOS and Windows-based utilities and commands/switches to diagnose and troubleshoot problems. Content may include the following:		
Windows-based tools:		
Conflict troubleshooter	9	466

11

REVIEW QUESTIONS

Circle True or False.

1. You can configure you desktop wallpaper via the Control Panel Accessories option.
    True / False

2. In the Windows 95 environment, the desktop includes the wallpapered area of your screen.
    True / False

3. Shortcuts in Widows 95 are configured the same way as shortcuts in Windows 3.x.
    True / False

4. The Start menu is a compilation of shortcuts. True / False

5. Describe how to create a new folder and add it to the Start menu.

    _____

    _____

    _____

    _____

    _____

6. Describe how to place a shortcut to My Computer in the Start menu.

    _____

    _____

    _____

    _____

    _____

CHAPTER TWELVE

UNDERSTANDING AND SUPPORTING WINDOWS NT WORKSTATION

LAB 12.1 UPGRADING TO WINDOWS NT WORKSTATION

Objective

The objective of this lab exercise is to allow you to use the upgrade path from Windows 3.x to Windows NT 4.0. After completing this lab exercise, you will be able to:

- Upgrade from Window 3.x to Windows NT 4.0 Workstation.
- Describe the upgrade path from Windows 3.x to Windows NT 4.0.

Materials Required

This lab exercise requires one complete lab workstation for every four students. The lab workstations should meet the following requirements:

- 486 or better
- 16MB of RAM
- Installation files for Windows NT Workstation

Lab Setup & Safety Tips

- Each lab workstation should have the Window 3.x operating system installed and functioning properly. Prior to the beginning of class, Windows NT installation files should be copied into a directory named C:\I386.

ACTIVITY

Upgrading to Windows NT Workstation

1. Power on your lab workstation and allow it to boot into Windows 3.x.
2. Open Program Manager.
3. Click the **File** menu.
4. Select **Run**.
5. Type **C:\I386\WINNT /B** and press **Enter**.
6. Press **Enter** when the copying is complete.
7. In the Program Manager, click **File** and select **Exit Windows**.
8. Click **OK** in the confirmation message box.
9. Power cycle your lab workstation.
10. Select the **NT Installation/Upgrade** option and press **Enter**.
11. Press the **Enter** key.
12. Press the **Page Down** key seven times through the license agreement.
13. Press the **F8** key to accept to the license agreement.
14. Press **Enter** to accept the detected hardware defaults.
15. Press **Enter**.
16. Press **Enter**.
17. Press **Enter** (this should restart your lab workstation).
18. Click the **Next** button.
19. Click the **Next** button.

20. Click the **Next** button.

21. Type your name and press **Enter**.

22. Type the product ID provided by your instructor, and press **Enter**.

23. Type a name for your lab workstation provided by your instructor, and press **Enter**.

24. Click the **Next** button.

25. Click the **Next** button.

26. Click the **Next** button.

27. Click the **Next** button.

28. Click the **Select From List** option button.

29. Select the **Msloopback adapter** and click the **OK** button.

30. Click the **Next** button.

31. Clear the **TCP/IP** check box and click the **NetBeui** check box.

32. Click the **Next** button.

33. Click the **Next** button.

34. Click the **Next** button.

35. Click the **Next** button.

36. Click the **Finish** button.

37. Select the proper time zone and click the **Close** button.

38. Click the **OK** button.

39. Click the **Test** button in the video display window.

40. Click the **Yes** button.

41. Click the **OK** button to close the video display window.

42. Click the **OK** button.

43. Insert the blank formatted floppy disk, and click the **OK** button.

44. Click the **Restart** button when prompted.

Lab Notes

Express Setup – Express Setup allows Windows NT to automatically install a group of preselected operating system components.

Custom Setup – Custom Setup allows you to select the components that you want to install.

REVIEW QUESTIONS

Circle True or False.

1. Windows NT does not include an upgrade path from Windows 95. True / False

2. Windows NT is Plug-and-Play compliant. True / False

3. Windows NT includes Express, Custom and Portable options similar to the Windows 95 setup program. True / False

4. Windows NT is a 16-bit operating system. True / False

5. The difference between upgrading and installing Windows NT is that an upgrade always takes less time. True / False

6. Jim wants to install Window NT on his PC. Jim has all of the necessary software but doesn't have a NIC. Does Jim have to purchase a NIC before proceeding with the Windows NT installation?

_____

_____

_____

_____

_____

LAB 12.2 INSTALLING WINDOWS NT WORKSTATION

Objective

The objective of this lab exercise is to allow you to install Windows NT Workstation. After completing this lab exercise, you will be able to:

- Install Windows NT Workstation.

- Create an emergency repair disk (ERD).

Materials Required

This lab exercise requires one complete lab workstation for every four students. The lab workstations should meet the following requirements:

- 486 or better
- 16MB of RAM
- CD-ROM drive

A set of Windows NT installation disks and an installation CD-ROM for each group of students.

Lab Setup & Safety Tips

- The following activity will erase all data stored on drive C.

ACTIVITY

12

Installing Windows NT Workstation

1. Insert the Windows NT installation Disk 1 and allow your system to boot from A drive.

2. Insert Disk 2 and press **Enter**.

3. Press **Enter**.

4. Press **Enter**.

5. Insert Disk 3 and press the **Enter** key.

6. Press the **Enter** key.

7. Press the **Page Down** button seven times.

8. Press the **F8** key.

9. Press the **Enter** key to accept the detected hardware defaults

10. Select the C drive and press the **Enter** key to install Windows NT.

11. Select the **Format the partition using the NTFS file system** option.

12. Press the F key.

13. Press **Enter** to accept the default directory.

14. Press **Enter** to continue.

15. Remove disk.

16. Press **Enter** to restart your computer.

17. Click the **Next** button.

18. Click the **Next** button.

19. Click the **Next** button.

20. Type your name and click the **Next** button.

21. Enter the product ID and click the **Next** button.

22. Enter a computer name and click the **Next** button.

23. Enter a password and click the **Next** button.

24. Click the **Next** button.

25. Click the **Next** button.

26. Click the **Next** button.

27. Select the **Do not connect this computer to a network at this time** option button.

28. Click the **Next** button.

29. Click the **Finish** button.

30. Select a time zone.

31. Click the **Close** button.

32. Click the **OK** button in the video display window

33. Click the **Test** button in the video display window.

34. Click the **Yes** button to verify the display settings.

35. Click the **OK** button to close the video display window.

36. Click the **OK** button.

37. Insert a floppy disk.

38. Click the **OK** button.

39. Click the **Restart** button.

Lab Notes

What is NTFS all about? – NTFS stands for New Technology file system. Unlike FAT or VFAT, NTFS includes security built right into the file system! NTFS always maintains a cluster size of 4K, which greatly reduces space commonly wasted by large FAT volumes. Note: Without special third-party software, an NTFS volume cannot be accessed from DOS.

FAT vs. VFAT? – FAT stands for file allocation table and is the file system that was introduced with MS-DOS. Since then Microsoft has updated FAT to be used in the Windows 95 environment; this update is VFAT. The V stands for Virtual. VFAT is an additional area in FAT reserved to store long filename information. Note that VFAT and FAT32 are not the same type of file system.

What is an ERD? – ERD stands for emergency repair disk. An ERD contains a backup copy of your Windows NT registry. Each ERD is designed specifically for the operating system that created it; ERDs are not interchangeable.

How do you make an ERD? – An ERD can be created during the Windows NT installation or at anytime after Windows NT has been installed. To create an ERD after Windows NT has been installed, click the Start button, point to Programs, and click Command Prompt. Type RDISK /S. The RDISK utility is used to create an ERD and the /S tells Windows NT not only to backup the registry files but also to include the Windows NT security file (SAM).

CERTIFICATION OBJECTIVES

A⁺

Table 12-1   DOS/Windows A+ objectives

Objective	Chapters	Page Numbers
1.6 Identify how the operating system stores information on the hard drive in file allocation tables. Content may include the following:		
Virtual File Allocation Table (VFAT)	5	205, 214
FAT32	12	594

REVIEW QUESTIONS

Circle True or False.

1. To install Windows NT you must have a network interface card. True / False

2. The Windows NT installation allows you the option to create and delete partitions.
   True / False

3. Windows NT allows you to configure a network interface card during the installation process.
   True / False

4. The Windows NT operating system does not support PCs that use a 486 processor.
   True / False

5. What is the name of the directory that contains the Windows NT installation files for x86 computers?

   _____

   _____

   _____

   _____

   _____

6. List the four questions that you will have to answer to install Windows NT.

   _____

   _____

   _____

   _____

   _____

12

LAB 12.3 CUSTOMIZING AND REPAIRING WINDOWS NT WORKSTATION

Objective

This lab exercise is designed to provide you the opportunity to configure some of the more commonly used settings in the Windows NT environment. After completing this lab exercise, you will be able to:

- Configure Windows NT to use customized shortcuts.
- Use an ERD to repair a Windows NT installation.
- View and modify the Boot.ini file.
- Install a printer driver in the Windows NT environment.

Materials Required

This lab exercise requires one complete lab workstation for every four students. The lab workstations should meet the following requirements:

- 486 or better
- 16MB of RAM
- A CD-ROM drive

The Windows NT workstation disks and CD-ROM

An ERD for each lab workstation

Lab Setup & Safety Tips

- Each lab workstation should have Windows NT installed and functioning properly.

ACTIVITY

Using shortcuts to manage memory

1. Right-click the desktop.
2. Select **New** from the menu.
3. Click **Shortcut**.
4. Type **C:\WINNT\WINFILE.EXE** and press **Enter**.
5. In the Select name of Shortcut box, type **File Manager**.
6. Click the **Finish** button.
7. Right-click on the newly created **File Manager** shortcut.
8. Select **Properties** from the menu.
9. Click the **Shortcut** tab.
10. Observe the location of the **Run in Separate Memory Space** check box.

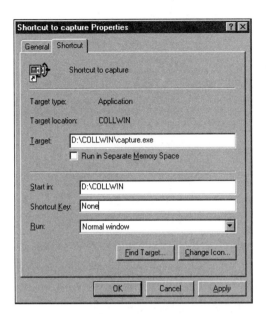

Figure 12-1 Properties box for a 16-bit Windows application

Using your textbook for reference answer the following questions:

1. How does Windows NT respond when the Run in Separate Memory Space check box is checked?

_____

_____

_____

_____

2. What does it mean when the Run in Separate Memory Space check box is grayed out?

_____

_____

_____

_____

Repairing a Windows NT installation

1. Insert the Windows NT installation Disk 1 and allow your system to boot from A drive.

2. Insert Disk 2 and press **Enter**.

3. Press **Enter**.

4. Press the letter **R** key.

5. Press **Enter**.

6. Press **Enter**.

7. Insert Disk 3 and press **Enter**.

8. Press the **Enter** key.

9. Press the **Enter** key.

10. Press the **Enter** key.

12

11. Insert the emergency repair disk.

12. Insert the Windows NT CD-ROM.

13. Press **Enter**.

Installing a printer driver

1. Power on your lab workstation and allow it to boot into Windows 95.

2. Double-click the **My Computer** icon.

3. Double-click the **Printers** folder

4. Double-click **Add New Printer**.

5. Click the **Next** button.

6. Choose the **My computer** option and click the **Next** button.

7. Choose the correct printer driver by first selecting the appropriate manufacturer and then printer model. Click the **OK** button when you are done.

8. Select the appropriate printer port and click the **Next** button.

9. Click the **Next** button again to use the default printer name.

10. Click the **Finish** button to complete the driver installatation.

Lab Notes

Repairing Windows NT – Windows NT includes a repair process as part of its setup program. Should a Windows NT installation become damaged or corrupt you can use the setup program to repair it.

REVIEW QUESTIONS

Circle True or False.

1. The Windows NT repair process can be used to reinstall Windows should it become damaged. True / False

2. An ERD is always necessary when using the emergency repair process. True / False

3. There must be a CD-ROM drive present to execute the emergency repair process. True / False

4. The Run in Separate Memory Space check box tells Windows NT to store that application in the swap file at all times. True / False

5. List two tasks that the Windows NT repair process can be used to accomplish.

_____

_____

_____

_____

_____

6. Janet's Windows NT workstation has been rendered useless by a virus. You are Janet's PC support technician and have cleaned the virus but the system still won't boot properly. Janet does not have an ERD. Describe how you could attempt to restore Janet's PC without reinstalling Windows NT.

_____

_____

_____

_____

LAB 12.4 THE WINDOWS NT REGISTRY

Objective

The objective of this lab exercise is to allow you to understand and modify the Windows NT registry. After completing this lab exercise, you will be able to:

- Name and describe some different values commonly used in the registry.

- Create and modify registry values.

Materials Required

This lab exercise requires one complete lab workstation for every four students. The lab workstation should meet the following requirements:

- 486 or better
- 16MB of RAM
- Windows NT Workstation

Lab Setup & Safety Tips

- Each lab workstation should have Windows NT installed and functioning properly.

ACTIVITY

Viewing the registry

1. Allow your lab workstation to boot into Windows NT.

2. Login to Windows NT.

3. Click the **Start** button.

4. Select **Run**.

5. Type **REGEDIT** and press **Enter**.

6. Using the registry editor, locate an example of each type of value, key and hive listed below. Write the path to each example on the lines provided.

Hive _____

_____

Key _____

_____

Binary value _____

_____

String value _____

_____

DWord value _____

_____

12

Modifying the right-click menu using the Registry Editor

1. Click the **Start** button.

2. Select **Run**.

3. Type **REGEDIT** and press **Enter**.

4. Double-click the **HKEY_LOCAL_MACHINE** hive.

5. Double-click the **Software** key.

6. Double-click the **Classes** key.

7. Double-click the **Directory** key.

8. Double-click the **Shell** key.

9. Click the **Edit** menu and point to **New**.

10. Click **Key**.

11. Type **File Manager** and press **Enter**.

12. Double-click the **File Manager** key.

13. Click the **Edit** menu and point to **New**.

14. Click **Key**.

15. Type **Command** and press **Enter**.

16. Look at the right window in the Registry Editor.

17. Locate the value **Default** (this is a string value).

18. Right-click the **Default** string value and select **Modify** from the menu.

19. Type **C:\WINNT\SYSTEM32\WINFILE.EXE**.

20. Click the **OK** button.

Testing your work

1. Right-click the **Start** button.

   There should now be a File Manager option on this menu.

2. Click the **File Manager** option.

   If your registry entries are completed correctly, File Manager will launch.

Lab Notes

Where is the Windows NT registry stored? – The Windows NT registry is stored in two centralized locations: C:\%systemroot%\system32\config and the user registry is stored in the user's personal profile.

What is the difference between REGEDIT and REGEDT32? – The REGEDIT utility has the ability to perform complex registry searches but does not include the ability to modify permissions of registry keys. REGEDT32 has the ability to modify permissions but does not include any type of registry search functions.

REVIEW QUESTIONS

Circle True or False.

1. Using the Registry Editor is an excellent way for beginning PC users to learn more about the operating system on their computer. True / False

2. REGEDIT can modify permissions. True / False

3. Windows NT stores its registry in one file called REG.DAT. True / False

4. One example of a key is HKEY_LOCAL_MACHINE. True / False

5. Windows NT stores each user's personal registry information in the user's profile directory. True / False

6. Jamie wants to use the Registry Editor to change her Netscape proxy configuration, but she is not that familiar with the Registry Editor utility. Describe below how Jamie could use the REGEDIT utility to search for her current proxy settings.

_____

_____

_____

_____

_____

12

MULTIMEDIA TECHNOLOGY

LABS INCLUDED IN THIS CHAPTER

LAB **13.1** MULTIMEDIA VIDEO

LAB **13.2** MULTIMEDIA SOUND

LAB **13.3** UNDERSTANDING LASER PRINTERS

LAB 13.1 MULTIMEDIA VIDEO

Objective

The objective of this lab exercise is to allow you to install and configure a video adapter card. After completing this lab exercise, you will be able to:

- Install a video adapter card.

- Install drivers for a video adapter card.

- Configure a video adapter card.

Materials Required

This lab exercise requires one complete lab workstation for every four students. The lab workstation should meet the following requirements:

- 486 or better
- 8MB of RAM
- Windows 95

One PCI video adapter for each lab workstation

Necessary drivers for each video adapter card

Tools necessary to remove the case and install a video adapter card

Lab Setup & Safety Tips

- Each lab workstation should have Windows 95 installed and functioning properly.

- Students must comply with standard ESD procedures.

- Always unplug the power cord before touching components in the case.

ACTIVITY

Installing the video adapter card

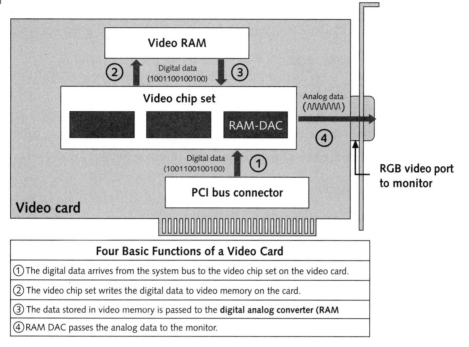

Figure 13-1   Four basic functions of a video card

1. Power off the lab workstation and unplug the power cord.

2. Remove the case from the lab workstation.

3. Locate an available PCI slot.

4. Remove the end-of-slot blank.

5. Gently slide the PCI expansion card into the PCI slot move the card from end to end until it is completely seated. Warning: Do not bend the card from side to side.

6. Plug in the power cord.

7. Stand clear of the case and power on the lab workstation. If you are able to view the POST screen, then the adapter has been properly installed.

8. Power off the lab workstation and unplug the power cord.

9. Replace the case.

10. Plug in the power cord.

11. Power on the lab workstation and allow it to boot into Windows 95.

Installing the video driver

1. Right-click the desktop.

2. Select **Properties** from the menu.

3. Click the **Settings** tab.

4. Click the **Change Display Adapter** button.

5. Click the **Change** button next to the Adapter Type heading.

6. Click the **Have Disk** button.

7. Insert the disk with the video drivers.

8. Click the **OK** button.

9. Select the video adapter driver that you want to use from the menu.

10. Click the **OK** button.

11. Click the **Close** button.

12. Click the **Close** button.

13. Click the **Yes** button when prompted to restart your computer.

Configuring the video adapter

1. Right-click the desktop.

2. Click the **Settings** tab.

3. Change the color palette to **256 colors**.

4. Change your display resolution to **1024 X 768**.

5. Click the **OK** button.

6. Click the **Yes** button when prompted to restart your computer.

Lab Notes

What is display resolution and dot pitch? – Display resolution is the measure of pixels on the screen that are addressable by software. Dot pitch is the distance between each adjacent pixel. The smaller the dot pitch, the closer together each pixel, and the more clear your image will appear.

Table 13-1 Features of a monitor

Monitor Characteristic	Description
Screen size	Screens are usually described as 14 inch, 16 inch, 17 inch, 21 inch, or larger. This screen size usually refers to the diagonal length of the lighted area, although the measurement is not particularly accurate. The actual diagonal is usually shorter than the advertised measurement.
Refresh rate	Refresh rate, or vertical scan rate, is the time it takes for an electronic beam to fill a video screen with lines from top to bottom. A Super VGA monitor must have a minimum refresh rate of 70 Hz or 70 times per second.
Interlaced	Rather than drawing the entire screen on every pass, interlaced monitors only refresh half the screen on every pass: the first pass draws the odd lines and the second pass draws even lines. Compared to noninterlaced monitors, interlaced monitors do not provide the same quality for the same refresh rate, although, because of interlacing, the overall effect is less noticeable.

Table 13-1   Some features of a monitor (continued)

Monitor Characteristic	Description
Dot pitch	Dot pitch is the distance between adjacent dots on the screen. The smaller the dot pitch, the higher the quality of the image. A high-quality monitor should have a dot pitch of no more than .28 mm.
Resolution	A measure of how many spots, or pixels, on the screen are addressable by software. The video controller card as well as the monitor must be capable of supporting the chosen resolution. A common resolution is 800 by 600. Resolutions are set from Control Panel in Windows.
Multiscan	Monitors that offer a variety of refresh rates are called multiscan monitors. Multiscan monitors can support different video cards, whereas fixed frequency monitors only support a single refresh rate.
Green monitor	A green monitor supports the EPA Energy Star program. When a screen saver is on, the monitor should use no more than 30 watts of electricity.

What is VRAM? – Video RAM, or VRAM, is RAM on a video card that allows simultaneous access from both the input and output processes.

What is WRAM? – WRAM is dual-ported video RAM that is faster and less expensive than VRAM. It has its own internal bus on the chip with a data path that is 256 bits wide.

CERTIFICATION OBJECTIVES

Table 13-2   DOS/Windows A+ objectives

Objective	Chapters	Page Numbers
3.2 Identify steps to perform an operating system upgrade. Content may include the following:		
Loading drivers	8, 11	389-391, 544
3.5 Interpret instructions and identify the procedures for loading/adding device drivers and the necessary software for certain devices. Content may include the following:		
Windows 3.x/Windows95 procedures	11	564

Table 13-3   Core A+ objectives

Objective	Chapters	Page Numbers
1.7 Identify proper procedures for installing and configuring peripheral devices. Content may include the following:		
Monitor/Video Card	4, 13, 14	175-178, 668, 672, 748
Associated drivers	2, 8	61, 389-391
2.1 Identify common symptoms and problems associated with each module and how to troubleshoot and isolate the problems. Content may include the following:		
Monitor/Video	7, App. E	352-356, E6
Device drivers	8	389-391

13

Table 13-3   Core A+ objectives (continued)

Objective	Chapters	Page Numbers
4.2 Identify the categories of RAM (Random Access Memory) terminology, their locations, and physical characteristics. Content may include the following: Terminology:		
VRAM (Video RAM)	9	430
WRAM (Windows Accelerator Card RAM)	13	672

REVIEW QUESTIONS

Circle True or False.

1. Video adapters normally use the PCI bus because it is faster than the ISA bus. True / False

2. All video cards have the same display capabilities. True / False

3. VRAM stands for Virtual RAM, which is commonly found on a video card. True / False

4. If Windows 95 doesn't have the video driver for your video adapter, you can install the correct video driver by using the Have Disk button. True / False

5. Describe the relationship between VRAM and your display resolution and color quality.

    _____

    _____

    _____

    _____

    _____

6. Jimmy has just installed a new video adapter, but now nothing will show on his monitor. Is Jimmy's problem hardware or software related? List the first three troubleshooting steps you would take if you were in Jimmy's position.

    _____

    _____

    _____

    _____

    _____

LAB 13.2 MULTIMEDIA SOUND

Objective

This lab exercise is designed to allow you to install and configure a sound card. After completing this lab exercise, you will be able to:

- Install a sound card.
- Install the proper device drivers for a sound card.

Materials Required

This lab exercise requires one complete lab workstation for every four students. The lab workstations should meet the following requirements:

- 486 or better
- 8MB of RAM
- Windows 95

One 8- or 16-bit sound card

One ESD mat

Grounding straps for each student

Documentation containing your sound card's jumper settings

Lab Setup & Safety Tips

- Each lab workstation should have Windows 95 installed.
- Verify that IRQ 5 and DMA 0 are available for use on all lab workstations.
- Students must comply with standard ESD procedures.
- Always unplug the power cord before touching components within the case.

ACTIVITY

Installing a sound card

1. Power off the lab workstation.

2. Unplug the power cord.

3. Remove the case from the lab workstation.

4. Locate an available ISA slot for the sound card.

5. Remove the end-of-slot blank.

6. Using the provided documentation, verify that the sound card jumpers are configured to use IRQ 5 and DMA 0.

7. Gently slide the PCI expansion card into the PCI slot move the card from end to end until it is completely seated. Warning: Do not bend the card from side to side.

8. Mount the sound card.

9. Replace the case.

10. Plug in the power cord.

11. Click the **Start** button, point to **Settings**, then click **Control Panel**.

12. Double-click the **Add New Hardware** icon.

13. Click the **Next** button three times and allow Windows 95 to detect your sound card.

14. When the process is complete, allow Windows to install the proper device driver.

If Windows does not detect the sound card

1. Click the **Start** button.

2. Point to **Settings** and click **Control Panel**.

3. Double-click the **Add New Hardware** icon.

4. Click the **Next** button.

5. Select the **No** option and then click the **Next** button.

6. Select the **Sound, video and game controller** option and then click the **Next** button.

7. Click the **Have Disk** button.

8. Insert the disk with the sound card drivers.

9. Click the **OK** button.

10. Select the sound card driver you want to use from the menu.

11. Click the **OK** button.

12. Click the **Next** button.

13. Click the **Finish** button.

14. Click the **Yes** button when you are prompted to restart your lab workstation.

Testing the sound card

1. Allow your lab workstation to boot into Windows 95.

2. Verify that your speakers are properly plugged in and powered on.

3. Click the **Start** button and select **Run**.

4. Type **C:\WINDOWS\CHIMES.WAV** and press **Enter**.

5. Click the **play arrow**, which points to the right.

Your workstation should respond by playing the chimes.wav file.

Lab Notes

What is a WAV file? – A WAV file is a sound file that is most commonly used to store multimedia sounds.

What is a MID file? – A MID, or MIDI, is a sound file that is most commonly used to store music.

What is the difference between an 8-bit and 16-bit sound card? – An 8-bit sound card uses 8 bits to store a sample value, and has a 256 sample size range. A 16-bit sound card uses 16-bits to store a sample value and has a sample size of up to 65,536.

CERTIFICATION OBJECTIVES

Table 13-4   Core A+ objectives

Objective	Chapters	Page Numbers
1.3 Identify available IRQs, DMA's, and I/O addresses and procedures for configuring them for device installation, including identifying switch and jumper settings. Content may include the following:		
Standard IRQ settings	3	123
Locating and setting switches/jumpers	2, 6, 8	52, 63, 263, 388, 403, 409
Sound Cards	8	385, 386
2.1 Identify common symptoms and problems associated with each module and how to troubleshoot and isolate the problems. Content may include the following:		
Sound Card/Audio	13	687

REVIEW QUESTIONS

Circle True or False.

1. An 8-bit sound card can produce a higher quality sound than a 16-bit sound card. True / False

2. All sound cards use a PCI bus. True / False

3. You can install a sound card's device driver by using the Add/Remove Programs icon in Control Panel. True / False

4. In order to use a sound card you must have a set of speakers or headphones. True / False

5. Most sound cards include a built-in microphone and speakers. True / False

6. Jacob just installed a new sound card into his Windows 95 PC. Windows did not detect the sound card when he used the Add New Hardware option in Control Panel. Below describe to Jacob how to install the proper sound card driver.

   _____

   _____

   _____

   _____

   _____

13

LAB 13.3 UNDERSTANDING LASER PRINTERS

Objective

The objective of this lab exercise is to allow you to inspect and understand the function of each component within a laser printer. After completing this lab exercise, you will be able to:

- Describe the function of each internal laser printer component.

- Describe the laser printing process.

Materials Required

This lab exercise requires one complete lab workstation for every four students. The lab workstation should meet the following requirements:

- 486 or better
- 8MB of RAM
- Windows 95

One functional laser printer for each lab workstation

One disassembled printer cartridge

Labels for each lab laser printer

Lab Setup & Safety Tips

- Each lab workstation should have Windows 95 installed and functioning properly.

- The instructor should be familiar with the lab laser printers.

- Students must comply with standard ESD procedures.

- Always unplug the power cord before touching components in the printer.

ACTIVITY

Inspecting and labeling a laser printer cartridge

1. Using the figure below, identify each of the components in the disassembled laser printer cartridge, and describe their functions on the lines provided.

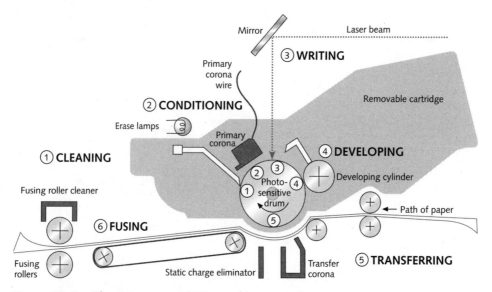

Figure 13-2 The six progressive steps of laser printing

Primary corona _____

_____

_____

Photo-sensitive drum _____

_____

_____

Developing cylinder _____

_____

_____

Inspecting and labeling a laser printer

1. Although all laser printers follow the same printing process, each of them has a different design. Your instructor will show you how to disassemble your lab workstation's laser printer in order to complete the following exercise.

2. Power off and unplug your laser printer.
   (If your laser printer has recently been used, allow it to cool before proceeding.)

3. Open your laser printer.

4. Identify each of the following laser printer components and describe its functionality:

Fuser _____

_____

_____

Paper tray _____

_____

_____

Primary corona wire _____

_____

_____

Transfer corona _____

_____

_____

Power supply _____

_____

_____

Sensors (all) _____

_____

_____

13

Expansion slots _____

_____

_____

Logic boards (all) _____

_____

_____

Lab Notes

The six steps of laser printing:

Step 1: Cleaning

Leftover toner from the previous image is scraped off the drum by the cleaning blade, and the previous electrostatic image is removed from the drum by an erase lamp.

Step 2: Conditioning

The primary corona applies a uniform negative charge (-600 volts) to prepare the drum for the new image. Warning: Do not expose the drum to light.

Step 3: Writing

- The PC sends the image to the formatter.
- The PC formatter sends the image to the DC controller.
- A laser beam is initiated and directed toward the scanning mirror.
- The laser beam reflects off of the scanning mirror and is focused by the focusing lens.
- The laser deflects off of the mirror and is projected through a slit into the removable cartridge.

Note that the speed of the drum motor and the speed of the scanning mirror motor are synchronized so that the laser beam completes one scanline and returns to the beginning of the drum.

Step 4: Developing

The electrostatic image is developed into a visible image when toner from a developer cylinder is transferred to the discharged (-100 volt) areas of the drum. The developer cylinder has a magnetic core that attracts the iron in the toner. As the cylinder rotates, the doctor blade keeps the toner at a uniform height. The toner acquires a negative charge by rubbing against the developer cylinder. This negative charge causes the toner to be attracted to the relatively positive (-100 volt) areas of the drum that have been exposed to the laser light.

Step 5: Transferring

The transfer corona produces a positive charge (+600 volts) on the back of the paper that pulls the toner off the drum to the paper. Once the toner is on the paper, a static charge eliminator reduces the paper's charge.

Step 6: Fusing

The toner is held on the paper by gravity and a weak electrostatic charge until it reaches the fuser assembly. Heat (180 C/356 F) and pressure applied by the fuser rollers melt the toner into the paper to produce a permanent image. Since the photo-sensitive drum is 3.75 inches in circumference, the print cycle must be repeated several times to print one sheet of paper. Note that, if the temperature rises above 410 F, the printer will automatically shut itself down to cool off the fuser.

What about ink jet printers?

As the print head moves across the paper, an electrical pulse flows through thin resistors at the bottom of all the chambers that the printer uses to form a character or image. The resistor in each chamber heats a thin layer of ink to more than $900°$ F to form a vapor bubble. As the vapor bubble expands, it pushes ink through the nozzle to transfer a drop of ink to the paper. A typical character is formed by an array of ink drops 20 across by 20 high.

CERTIFICATION OBJECTIVES

Table 13-5   Core A+ objectives

Objective	Chapters	Page Numbers
3.3 Identify the potential hazards and proper safety procedures relating to lasers and high voltage equipment.		
Lasers can cause blindness	13	690
High voltage equipment can cause electrocution, e.g.,	7	334
5.1 Identify basic concepts, printer operations, printer components, and field replaceable units in primary printer types. Content may include the following:		
Types of Printers:		
Laser	13, App. E, 7	357-360, 690, E8-9
Inkjet	7, 13	360-361, 695
Paper feeder mechanisms	7	359
Common Field Replaceable Units (FRUs) for printers include:		
Primary Power Supply Boards or Assemblies	13	690-695
High Voltage Power Supplies	13	690-695
System (or Main Logic) Boards	13	690-695
Sub Logic Boards	13	690-695
Motors (main drive, paper feed, transport, etc.)	13	690-695
Fusers	13	690-695
Rollers	13	690-695
Sensors	13	690-695
Switches	13	690-695
Cables	13	690-695
Printheads/laser devices	13	690-695
EPROMs	9	430
Operator Panels	13	690-695
Gear Packs	13	690-695
5.2 Identify care and service techniques and common problems with primary printer types. Content may include the following:		
Feed and output	7, App. E	360, E8-10
Paper jam	7, App. E	359, E8-10
Print quality	7, App. E	360-361, E8-10

13

REVIEW QUESTIONS

Circle True or False.

1. The photo-sensitive drum is always housed within the printer cartridge. True / False

3. The primary corona is always housed within the fuser. True / False

3. The erase lamp melts excess ink off of the photo-sensitive drum. True / False

4. During the printing process, mirrors are used to control the movement of a tiny laserbeam. True / False

5. The primary corona wire is a small wire that should be attached between the primary corona and fuser. True / False

6. All laser printers use only one motor. True / False

7. What are the six steps of the laser printing process?

_____

_____

_____

_____

_____

8. Describe how to replace the fuser in your lab workstation.

_____

_____

_____

_____

_____

PURCHASING A PC
OR BUILDING YOUR OWN

LAB 14.1 BUILDING A NEW PC: PART 1

Objective

The objective of this lab exercise is for you to begin building a PC. This lab exercise will combine the skills you have learned in previous exercises and allow you more hands-on time to further develop your hardware skills. After completing this lab exercise, you will be able to:

- Install a systemboard.
- Install a CPU.
- Install RAM.

Materials Required

For this lab exercise, students need the tools necessary to complete the installation of the following components:

One PC case

One Pentium systemboard

Two 4MB SIMMS

One Pentium CPU

One CPU cooling fan

Thermal grease

Lab Setup & Safety Tips

- Students must comply with standard ESD procedures.
- Students should have documentation describing the correct systemboard jumper and DIP switch settings for the CPU that is to be used for this activity.
- Before beginning these activities, students should verify and, if necessary, reconfigure the systemboard to use the proper jumper and DIP switch settings.

ACTIVITY

Installing the CPU

1. Place the systemboard on the ESD mat.
2. Remove the CPU from its package, and note the blunt end on the processor.
3. Locate the ZIF on the systemboard and unlatch the lever.
4. Install the CPU by first matching the blunt end of the ZIF with the blunt end of the CPU and then pressing gently down on the CPU.
5. Don't force the CPU. If it is not moving into place with ease, check for bent pins on the bottom of the CPU. Also verify that you have it lined up properly with the ZIF.
6. Lock the CPU into position using the ZIF lever.
7. Coat the bottom of the CPU fan with thermal grease.
8. Place the CPU fan on top of the CPU.
9. Lock the CPU fan into position.

Installing the RAM

1. Locate the SIMM banks on your systemboard.

2. Place the first SIMM at a 45° angle and gently slide it into bank zero.

3. Slowly push the SIMM upright until it snaps into position.

4. Repeat the Steps 1, 2, and 3 for bank 1.

Mounting the systemboard

The process of mounting a systemboard varies from PC to PC because of the different case designs available. The following attempts to discuss some of the commonalties between cases.

1. Locate the screws and standoffs necessary for mounting your systemboard.

2. Line up the systemboard with the case to determine where the screws and standoffs will be placed.

   Note: Any screws used must be placed within an area on the systemboard that allow for metal to metal contact. If you are unsure, consult the systemboard user's manual.

3. Install the standoffs.

4. Mount the systemboard and lock the standoffs into place, if necessary.

5. Secure any and all screws.

6. Locate the P8 and P9 power connectors.

7. Attach the P8 and P9 power connectors. Be sure the black wires of each connector are placed side-by-side.

Lab Notes

What voltage is my CPU? – Different types of CPUs use different voltage settings. Consult your CPU support documentation for details. Note: Some CPUs will have the voltage written on the top of the CPU.

What divisor should I use? – The divisor varies from system to system. Consult your support documentation for the systemboard and the CPU for more details.

CERTIFICATION OBJECTIVES

Table 14-1   Core A+ objectives

Objective	Chapters	Page Numbers
1.2 Identify basic procedures for adding and removing field replaceable modules. Examples of modules:		
System board	14	728
Power supply	10	498-500
Processor / CPU	14	719
Memory	9, 14	473, 722

14

REVIEW QUESTIONS

Circle True or False

1. Systemboards are designed to use specific types of CPUs. True / False

2. Memory must always be installed at the same time as the CPU. True / False

3. Standoffs are used to keep the systemboard from touching the case and shorting the entire PC. True / False

4. All systemboards require a minimum of 8 screws. True / False

5. The P8 and P9 power connectors are used to supply power to the systemboard. True / False

6. One of your coworkers, Joe, is attempting to install a CPU. After several attempts Joe has decided to call you for help. Describe to Joe how to identify which direction the CPU should be installed.

_____

_____

_____

_____

_____

7. Which banks must always be included when installing RAM and why?

_____

_____

_____

_____

_____

LAB 14.2 BUILDING A NEW PC: PART 2

Objective

The objective of this lab exercise is to continue building the PC begun in Lab 14.1. This lab exercise will allow you to further develop your hardware installation and configuration skills. After completing this lab exercise you will be able to:

- Install COM and LPT ports.
- Install a hard drive.
- Install a CD-ROM drive.
- Install a floppy drive.

Materials Required

The partial lab workstation from lab exercise 14.1

One Cable Select data cable

One hard drive

One CD-ROM drive

The COM and LPT ports included with the systemboard

One floppy drive

The tools necessary to complete the installation of the of the previously listed components

Lab Setup & Safety Tips

- Students should have documentation describing the jumper settings for the hard drive and CD-ROM drive prior to starting the activity.
- Students must comply with standard ESD procedures.

ACTIVITY

Installing the COM and LPT ports

1. Locate the COM and LPT ports that were packaged with the systemboard.
2. Locate two available expansion slots within the case (you will not need any available expansion slots on the systemboard).
3. Remove any blanks that might be in place.
4. Locate the pins for the LPT cable.
5. Attach the LPT cable to the systemboard. Be sure that pin one is aligned with the red stripe on the data cable.
6. Slide the LPT port into place and secure it with a screw.
7. Locate the pins for the COM ports.
8. Attach the COM port cables to the systemboard. Be sure that the pins are aligned correctly.
9. Slide the COM ports into place and secure them with a screw.

14

Installing the hard drive

1. Locate an available bay for the hard drive.

2. Remove any blanks that might be in place.

3. Slide the hard drive into the bay.

4. Jumper the hard drive to the cable select position.

5. Connect the IDE data cable to the systemboard. Be sure to verify that the red line on the data cable is matched with the pin 1 marking on the systemboard.

6. Connect the IDE data cable and the power connector. Note that the hard drive should be attached to the IDE connector closest to the systemboard.

7. Mount the hard drive.

Installing the CD-ROM drive

1. Locate an available bay for the CD-ROM drive.

2. Remove any blanks that might be in place.

3. Slide the CD-ROM drive into the bay.

4. Jumper the CD-ROM drive to the cable select position.

5. Connect the IDE data cable and the power connector. Note that the CD-ROM drive should be attached to the IDE connector farthest from the systemboard.

6. Mount the CD-ROM drive.

Installing the floppy drive

1. Locate an available 3.5 drive bay.

2. Remove any blanks that might be in place.

3. Slide the 3.5 floppy drive into the bay.

4. Plug in the data cable.

5. Plug in the power connector.

Lab Notes

I/O ports – This lab exercise assumes that both the COM and LPT ports were included with the systemboard at the time of purchase. Note that this is not always the case and, at times, you may need to purchase a separate I/O card.

CERTIFICATION OBJECTIVES

Table 14-2 Core A+ objectives

Objective	Chapters	Page Numbers
1.2 Identify basic procedures for adding and removing field replaceable modules. Examples of modules:		
Storage devices	6, 14	261-267, 733-739
Input devices	14	732
Output devices	14	732, 753
1.5 Identify proper procedures for installing and configuring IDE/EIDE devices. Content may include the following:		
Master/slave	6	263, 264
Devices per channel	6	264
1.7 Identify proper procedures for installing and configuring peripheral devices. Content may include the following:		
Storage devices	14	736

REVIEW QUESTIONS

Circle True or False.

1. COM ports don't follow the pin one rule. True / False

2. Cable Select is the same as master and slave. True / False

3. CD-ROMs must always be slave. True / False

4. A CD-ROM should not be mounted next to a hard drive because it has a magnetic field that could erase data off of the hard drive. True / False

5. List three ways an IDE CD-ROM could be jumpered to function properly with only one other hard drive present.

_____

_____

_____

_____

_____

6. How, if at all, are the COM ports affected when a systemboard's LPT port is an embedded component?

_____

_____

_____

_____

_____

14

LAB 14.3 BUILDING A NEW PC: PART 3

Objective

The objective of this lab exercise is to complete building the PC that you began in Labs 14.1 and 14.2. This lab exercise will allow you to further develop your hardware installation and configuration skills. After completing this lab exercise, you will be able to:

- Install a video card.

- Install a sound card.

- Install a network card.

- Describe how resources are allocated throughout your PC.

- Complete the final PC configuration steps and describe the value of allowing a system burn-in period.

Materials Required

The partial lab workstation from lab exercise 14.2

One PCI video card

One 16-bit ISA sound card

One network interface card

The tools necessary to complete the installation of the previously listed components

Lab Setup & Safety Tips

- Students must comply with standard ESD procedures.

- The student should receive documentation describing the jumper settings for the sound card and the network interface card prior to starting the activity.

ACTIVITY

Installing the video card

1. Locate the PCI video card.

2. Locate one available PCI expansion slot.

3. Remove any blanks that may be in place.

4. Gently slide the video card into the PCI slot. Be careful not to bend the video card from side to side.

5. Secure the video card with a screw.

Installing the sound card

1. Locate the sound card

2. Write down your sound card's jumper configuration and verify that it is not conflicting with any other devices.

_____

_____

_____

3. Locate one available ISA expansion slot.

4. Remove any blanks that might be in place.

5. Gently slide the sound card into the ISA slot. Be careful not to bend the video card from side to side.

6. Secure the sound card with a screw.

Installing the network interface card

1. Locate the network interface card.

2. Write down your network card's jumper configuration, and verify that it is not conflicting with any other devices.

_____

_____

_____

3. Locate one available ISA expansion slot.

4. Remove any blanks that may be in place.

5. Gently slide the network card into the ISA slot. Be careful not to bend the video card from side to side.

6. Secure the network card with a screw.

Completing your resources worksheet

On the lines below, record the resources used by each device.

COM1 _____

COM2 _____

LPT1 _____

LPT2 _____

Sound card _____

_____

Network card _____

_____

Completing the final steps

1. Thoroughly inspect the case, looking for loose wires and any metal (screws, blanks, etc.) that could cause a short.

2. Replace the top to the case.

3. Plug in the monitor.

4. Plug in the keyboard.

5. Plug in the mouse.

6. Secure LAN line (if available).

7. Connect speakers (if available).

8. Connect all power cords.

14

9. Power on the PC for the first time.

10. Enter the CMOS setup program.

11. Set the date and time.

12. Set the correct configuration for each of the hardware components.

13. Save your changes and reboot.

14. Install an operating system.

15. Allow at least 24 hours for a system burn-in period.

Lab Notes

How do I modify the resources of an integrated network card? – When network cards are integrated, you can modify their resources by using the CMOS setup program.

What is system burn in? – The term system burn in refers to the testing of new hardware. After a PC has been assembled and each component has been tested for functionality, most technicians allow the system at least a 24-hour burn in period. During the system burn in period, the computer is left powered on with an operating system installed and configured properly. Many times new hardware components will show their faults during the first 24 to 48 hours of use, the system burn in period is used to detect these faults before the computer is released to a customer.

CERTIFICATION OBJECTIVES

Table 14-3   Core A+ objectives

Objective	Chapters	Page Numbers
1.3 Identify available IRQs, DMA's, and I/O addresses and procedures for configuring them for device installation, including identifying switch and jumper settings. Content may include the following:		
Standard IRQ settings	3	123
Differences between jumpers and switches	2, 6	52, 263
Locating and setting switches/jumpers	2, 6, 8	52, 63, 263, 388, 403, 409
Sound Cards	8	385, 386
Network Cards	1	8-9
1.7 Identify proper procedures for installing and configuring peripheral devices. Content may include the following:		
Monitor/Video Card	4, 13, 14	175-178, 668, 672, 748
1.9 Identify procedures for upgrading BIOS.		
Upgrade system hardware	3	101, 102
4.4 Identify the purpose of CMOS (Complementary Metal-Oxide Semiconductor), what it contains and how to change its basic parameters. Example Basic CMOS Settings:		
Network interface card	3	120-121

REVIEW QUESTIONS

Circle True or False.

1. You must always install the video card before the sound card. True / False

2. Most sound cards use IRQ 9 by default. True / False

3. All network interface cards require DMA 3. True / False

4. PCI video cards are faster than ISA video cards. True / False

5. Before powering on a system, you should always look for loose wires or metal pieces. True / False

6. Name three CMOS settings that must be modified after a PC is powered on for the first time.

_____

_____

_____

_____

_____

7. Describe how a system burn in period affects a product's quality.

_____

_____

_____

_____

_____

14

CHAPTER FIFTEEN

COMMUNICATING OVER PHONE LINES

LABS INCLUDED IN THIS CHAPTER

LAB 15.1 COMMUNICATIONS AND DOS/WINDOWS 3.x

LAB 15.2 COMMUNICATIONS AND WINDOWS 95

LAB 15.3 COMMUNICATIONS AND WINDOWS NT

LAB 15.4 MODEM TROUBLESHOOTING

LAB 15.1 COMMUNICATIONS AND DOS/WINDOWS 3.x

Objective

The objective of this lab exercise is to allow you to install and configure an AT-compatible modem. After completing this lab exercise, you will be able to:

- Install an internal modem.
- Use AT commands to control a modem.
- Use the Windows 3.x Terminal program.

Materials Required

This lab exercise requires one complete lab workstation for every four students. The lab workstations should meet the following requirements:

- 486 or better
- 4MB of RAM
- Windows 3.x

One internal modem

One analog phone line for each lab workstation

One ESD mat

Grounding straps for each student

Tools necessary to remove the case and install an internal modem

Lab Setup & Safety Tips

- Students must comply with standard ESD procedures.
- Students should have documentation describing the jumper settings for the internal modem prior to beginning the activities.

ACTIVITY

Installing a modem

1. Power off and unplug your lab workstation.

2. Remove the case.

3. Locate an available ISA slot for the internal modem.

4. Remove any blanks that might be in place.

5. Configure the modem's jumpers to use an available COM port.

6. Gently install the modem into the ISA slot. Warning: Be careful not to bend the modem from side to side.

7. Secure the modem with a screw.

8. Plug in the lab workstation.

9. Stand clear of the lab workstation and power it on.

10. Enter the CMOS setup program.

11. Verify that the modem is not conflicting with an existing COM port.

12. If the modem is conflicting with a COM port, disable the COM port.

13. Save your changes and reboot the PC.

14. Power off your lab workstation.

15. Unplug the power cord.

16. Replace the case.

17. Plug in the power cord.

18. Power on your lab workstation and allow it to boot into Windows 3.x.

Dialing with Terminal

1. Double-click the **Accessories** group icon.

2. Double-click the **Terminal** icon. (If you have not run Terminal on this PC before, a window will open; click the **Cancel** button to close the window.)

3. Click the **Settings** menu.

4. Click the **Communications** option.

5. Configure the Terminal program to use the following settings:

   Baud rate: 19200

   Data bits: 8

   Parity: None

   Flow Control: Xon/Xoff

   Stop bits: 1

   Connector: (choose the COM port of the installed modem)

6. Click the **OK** button.

7. Click the **Phone** menu.

8. Select **Dial**.

9. Type the phone number you want to dial.

10. Click the **OK** button.

11. Click the **Phone** menu.

12. Select **Hangup**.

Using AT commands

1. Double-click the **Accessories** group icon.

2. Double-click the **Terminal** icon.

3. Click the **Settings** menu.

4. Click the **Communications** option.

5. Configure the Terminal program to use the following settings:

   Baud rate: 19200

   Data bits: 8

   Parity: None

15

Flow Control: Xon/Xoff

Stop bits: 1

Connector: (choose the COM port of the installed modem)

6. Click the **OK** button.

7. In the Terminal window, type **ATZ** and press **Enter** (this command is used to reset the modem).

8. Type **ATDT** ######## (represents a phone number you want to dial).

9. Press **Enter**.

10. Type **ATH** and press **Enter** (this will hang up the phone).

11. Type **ATZ** and press **Enter**.

Table 15-1   Some examples of AT commands

Command	Description
ATDT 5552115	Dial the given number using tone dialing.
ATDP 5552115	Dial the given number using pulse dialing.
ATD 9,5552115	Dial 9 and pause, then dial the remaining numbers (use this method to get an outside line from a business phone).
AT &F1DT9,5552115	Restore the default factory settings. Dial using tone dialing. Pause after dialing the 9. Dial the remaining numbers.
ATM2L2	Always have the speaker on. Set loudness of speaker at medium.
ATI3	Report the modem ROM version.

Table 15-2   AT commands for Hayes-compatible modems

Command	Description	Some Values and Their Meanings
+++	**Escape sequence:** Tells the modem to return to command mode. You should pause at least 1 second before you begin the sequence. After you end it, wait another second before you send another command. Don't begin this command with AT.	
On	**Go online:** Tells the modem to return to online data mode. This is the reverse command from the escape sequence above.	O0 Return online O1 Return online and retrain (perform training or handshaking again with the remote modem)
A/	**Repeat last command:** Repeat the last command performed by the modem. Don't begin the command with AT, but do follow it with Enter. Useful when redialing a busy number.	
In	**Identification:** Instructs the modem to return product identification information.	I0 Return the product code I3 Return the modem ROM version
Zn	**Reset:** Instructs the modem to reset and restore the configuration to that defined at power on.	Z0 Reset and return to user profile 0 Z1 Reset and return to user profile 1
&F	**Factory default:** Instructs the modem to reload the factory default profile. In most cases, use this command to reset the modem rather than the Z command.	

Table 15-2   AT commands for Hayes-compatible modems (continued)

Command	Description	Some Values and Their Meanings
A	**Answer the phone:** Instructs the modem to answer the phone, transmit the answer tone, and wait for a carrier from the remote modem.	
Dn	**Dial:** Tells the modem to dial a number. There are several parameters that can be added to this command. A few are listed on the right.	D5551212 Dial the given number D, Causes the dialing to pause DP Use pulse dialing DT Use tone dialing DW Wait for dial tone D& Wait for the credit card dialing tone before continuing with the remaining dial string
Hn	**Hang up:** Tells the modem to hang up.	H0 Hang up H1 Hang up and enter command mode
Mn	**Speaker control:** Instructs the modem as to how it is to use its speaker.	M0 Speaker always off M1 Speaker on until carrier detect M2 Speaker always on
Ln	**Loudness:** Sets the loudness of the modem's speaker.	L1 Low L2 Medium L3 High
Xn	**Response:** Tells the modem how it is to respond to a dial tone and busy signal.	X0 Blind dialing; the modem does not need to hear the dial tone first and will not hear a busy signal X4 Modem must first hear the dial tone and responds to a busy signal (this is the default value)

15

Lab Notes

What are AT commands? – AT commands are a set of standardized modem commands that all Hayes-compatible modems can understand.

CERTIFICATION OBJECTIVES

Table 15-3   Core A+ objectives

Objective	Chapters	Page Numbers
1.1 Identify basic terms, concepts, and functions of system modules, including how each module should work during normal operation. Examples of concepts and modules:		
Modem	1, 15	8, 763
BIOS	1, 2, 3	6, 56, 61, 99-105
CMOS	1, 2, 3	7, 51-53, 120
1.2 Identify basic procedures for adding and removing field replaceable modules. Examples of modules:		
Modem	14	742-745

Table 15-3 Core A+ objectives (continued)

Objective	Chapters	Page Numbers
1.3 Identify available IRQs, DMA's, and I/O addresses and procedures for configuring them for device installation, including identifying switch and jumper settings. Content may include the following:		
Standard IRQ settings	3	123
Differences between jumpers and switches	2, 6	52, 263
Locating and setting switches/jumpers	2, 6, 8	52, 63, 263, 388, 403, 409
Modems	15	765
1.7 Identify proper procedures for installing and configuring peripheral devices. Content may include the following:		
Modem	14	742

Table 15-4 DOS/Windows A+ objectives

Objective	Chapters	Page Numbers
5.2 Identify concepts and capabilities relating to the Internet and basic procedures for setting up a system for Internet access. Content may include the following:		
Dial-up access	16	832
Configuring modem	15	785

REVIEW QUESTIONS

Circle True or False.

1. A modem could never conflict with a COM port. True / False

2. The Terminal program can be used to test a modem. True / False

3. ATDT and ATZ are examples of ATS commands. True / False

4. The ATDT command is used to reset an AT-compatible modem. True / False

5. How should an AT-compatible modem respond to the ATH command?

    _____

    _____

    _____

    _____

    _____

6. Write the AT commands necessary to reset, dial, and hang up an AT-compatible modem.

    _____

    _____

    _____

    _____

    _____

LAB 15.2 COMMUNICATIONS AND WINDOWS 95

OBJECTIVE

The objective of this lab exercise is to allow you to install and configure all of the necessary components to create a functional Dial-Up Networking connection in Windows 95. After completing this lab exercise, you will be able to:

- Install Dial-Up Networking.

- Install a modem device driver.

- Install the dial-up adapter.

- Configure Windows 95 to use a PPP dial-up connection.

Materials Required

This lab exercise requires one complete lab workstation for every four students. The lab workstations should meet the following requirements:

- 486 or better
- 8MB of RAM
- Windows 95

One internal modem

Lab Setup & Safety Tips

- Each lab workstation should have Windows 95 installed and functioning properly.

ACTIVITY

Installing Dial-Up Networking

1. Power on your lab workstation and allow it to boot into Windows 95.

2. Click the **Start** button.

3. Point to **Settings**.

4. Click **Control Panel**.

5. Double-click the **Add/Remove Programs** icon.

6. Click the **Windows Setup** tab.

7. Double-click **Communications**.

8. Click the **Dial-Up Networking** check box to select it.

9. Click the **OK** button.

10. Click the **OK** button.

11. If prompted, enter the path to the installation files.

15

Installing a modem driver

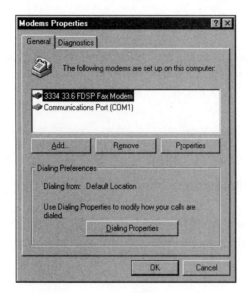

Figure 15-1 Maximum modem speed often included in the modem name
(in this case 33.6 Kbps)

1. Click the **Start** button.

2. Point to **Settings**.

3. Click **Control Panel**.

4. Double-click the **Modems** icon.

5. If you are not prompted to install a modem, click the **Add** button.

6. Click the **Next** button (this will allow Windows 95 to search for a modem).

7. Verify that Windows 95 has detected the correct type of modem.

8. Click the **Next** button.

9. Click the **Finish** button.

10. Click the **OK** button.

Installing the dial-up adapter

This exercise assumes that you do not have any networking components installed. Prior to beginning this activity, remove any networking components that might be present.

1. Click the **Start** button.

2. Point to **Settings**.

3. Click **Control Panel**.

4. Double-click the **Network** icon.

5. Click the **Add** button.

6. Double-click **Client**.

7. Select **Microsoft** from Manufacturer list.

8. Double-click the **Client for Microsoft Networks** option.

9. Select **Microsoft** from the Manufacturer list.

10. Double-click the **Dial-Up Adapter** option.

11. Click the **Add** button.

12. Double-click the **Protocol** option.

13. Select **Microsoft** from Manufacturer list.

14. Double-click the **TCP/IP** option.

15. Click the **OK** button.

16. If prompted, enter the path to the installation files.

17. Click the **Yes** button when prompted to restart your computer.

Creating and configuring a dialer

1. Double-click the **My Computer** icon.

2. Double-click the **Dial-Up Networking** icon.

3. Double-click **Make New Connection**.

4. Type **LAB DIALER** in the Type a Name for the Computer You Are Dialing box, and click the **Next** button.

5. Type **555–5555** in the Telephone Number box.

6. Click the **Next** button.

7. Click the **Finish** button.

8. In the Dial-up Networking window, right-click the **LAB DIALER** icon.

9. Select **Properties** from the menu.

10. Click the **Server Type** button.

11. Verify that the type of dial-up server is set to the **PPP Windows 95, Windows NT 3.5, Internet** option.

12. Deselect the NetBuei and the IPX/SPX check boxes from the **Allowed Network Protocols** list.

13. Click the **TCP/IP** button.

14. Click the **Specify Name Server Addresses** option button.

15. Type **127.15.8.4** in the primary DNS box (this is a fictional DNS address).

16. Type **127.15.8.5** in the secondary DNS box (this is a fictional DNS address).

17. Click the **OK** button.

18. Click the **OK** button again.

19. Click **OK** one last time.

LAB NOTES

What is the difference between the modem driver and the dial-up adapter? – You install a modem driver using the Modems option in Control Panel. The modem driver ensures proper communication between the operating system and the modem's hardware. The dial-up adapter is a dial-up networking component that is not necessary to use the modem but is necessary to connect using some protocols such as PPP.

What is a dialer? – A dialer is a Windows 95 object that contains settings for a particular dial-up connection, such as phone numbers, IP addresses, and allowed protocols. In Windows 95 you can create and configure multiple dialers, each of which can contain a different configuration.

15

CERTIFICATION OBJECTIVES

Table 15-5   DOS/Windows A+ objectives

Objective	Chapters	Page Numbers
5.2 Identify concepts and capabilities relating to the Internet and basic procedures for setting up a system for Internet access. Content may include the following:		
Dial-up access	16	832
Configuring modem	15	785

REVIEW QUESTIONS

Circle True or False.

1. Dial-Up Networking is installed via the Add New Hardware option found in the Control Panel. True / False

2. Modem drivers are installed using the Modems option in the Control Panel. True / False

3. All dialers must be configured to dial the same phone number. True / False

4. Dialers are created using the Make New Connection option in the Dial-Up Networking folder. True / False

5. Joy has just purchased and installed a new modem. Joy has Windows 95 installed on her PC. What should Joy do next to allow her operating system to properly communicate with her modem?

_____

_____

_____

_____

6. List four configurable options in a Windows 95 dialer.

_____

_____

_____

_____

LAB 15.3 COMMUNICATIONS AND WINDOWS NT

OBJECTIVE

The objective of this lab exercise is to allow you to install and configure all of the necessary components to create a functional Dial-Up Networking connection using the Remote Access Service. After completing this lab exercise you will be able to:

- Install a modem device driver.
- Install the remote access service (RAS).
- Configure Windows NT to use a PPP dial-up connection.

Materials Required

This lab exercise requires one complete lab workstation for every four students. The lab workstations should meet the following requirements:

- 486 or better
- 16MB of RAM
- Windows NT
- One internal modem

Lab Setup & Safety Tips

- Each lab workstation should have Windows NT installed and functioning properly.

ACTIVITY

Installing a modem driver

1. Power on your lab workstation and allow it to boot into Windows NT.
2. Log on to your Windows NT system.
3. Click the **Start** button.
4. Point to **Settings**.
5. Click **Control Panel**.
6. Double-click the **Modems** icon.
7. If you are not prompted to install a modem, click the **Add** button.
8. Click the **Next** button (this will allow Windows NT to search for a modem).
9. Verify that Windows NT has detected the correct type of modem.
10. Click the **Next** button.
11. Click the **Finish** button.
12. Click the **OK** button.

15

Installing the RAS

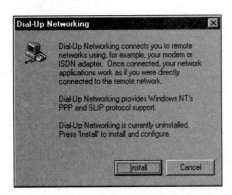

Figure 15-2   Dial-Up Networking installation

1. Double-click the **My Computer** icon.

2. When prompted, click the **Install** button.

3. If prompted, enter the path to the installation files.

4. Using the drop-down arrow, select the modem you have previously installed.

5. Click the **OK** button.

6. Click the **Network** button and select the **TCP/IP** check box.

7. Click the **OK** button.

8. Click the **Configure** button.

9. Verify that the **Dial Out Only** option button is selected.

10. Click the **OK** button.

11. Click the **Continue** button.

12. Click the **Restart** button when prompted to restart your computer.

Creating and configuring a RAS connection

1. Double-click the **My Computer** icon.

2. Double-click the **Dial-Up Networking** icon.

3. Click the **OK** button.

4. Select the **I know all about phonebook entries** check box, and click the **Finish** button.

5. In the phone number box, type **555-5555**.

6. Click the **Server** tab.

7. Click the **Specify name server addresses** option button.

8. Type **127.15.8.4** in the primary DNS box (this is a fictional DNS address).

9. Type **127.15.8.5** in the secondary DNS box (this is a fictional DNS address).

10. Click the **OK** button.

11. Click the **Security** tab.

12. Click the **Accept any authentication including clear text** option button.

13. Click the **OK** button.

Lab Notes

How do I uninstall RAS? – To uninstall RAS, access the Network icon via the Control Panel, and then click the Services tab. To completely remove RAS, select RAS by clicking on it and then clicking the Remove button.

REVIEW QUESTIONS

Circle True or False.

1. Configuring a dialer in Windows 95 is the same as configuring a dialer in Windows NT. True / False

2. Windows NT will attempt to detect your modem after it has been installed. True / False

3. RAS is used to create and configure remote access connections. True / False

4. You can uninstall RAS via the Add/Remove icon in the Control Panel. True / False

5. RAS can be configured to dial out or receive calls. True / False

6. A phone book entry is the Windows NT's version of a dialer. True / False

7. Neil wants to configure his Windows NT computer to dial into the Internet but doesn't know where in Windows NT to type the DNS and WINS addresses. Describe where in Windows NT Neil must go to enter the DNS and WINS addresses for his remote connection.

_____

_____

_____

_____

_____

15

LAB 15.4 MODEM TROUBLESHOOTING

OBJECTIVE

The objective of this lab exercise is to allow you hands-on time to troubleshoot Dial-Up Networking problems in both Windows 95 and Windows NT. After completing this lab exercise, you will be able to:

- Troubleshoot modem communications in Windows 95.

- Troubleshoot modem communications in Windows NT.

Materials Required

This lab exercise requires one complete lab workstation for every four students. The lab workstations should meet the following requirements:

- 486 or better
- 16MB of RAM
- Windows 95 and Windows NT
- One internal modem

Lab Setup & Safety Tips

- Each lab workstation should be dual booted with the Windows 95 and Windows NT operating systems.

- During the following lab exercises, students are required to dial out using their modems. Note that an analog line for each lab workstation is not necessary. Students must be able to at least make the modem dial by clearing the Wait for dial tone before dialing check box. Note that this option is available in both Windows 95 and Windows NT.

ACTIVITY

Troubleshooting modem communications in Windows 95

The following steps should be performed while Student 2 is away from the lab workstation.

Student 1

1. Power on your lab workstation and allow it to boot into Windows 95.

2. Click the **Start** button.

3. Point to **Settings**.

4. Click **Control Panel**.

5. Double-click the **System** icon.

6. Click the **Device Manager** tab.

7. Double-click the **Modems** icon.

8. Double-click the installed modem.

9. Deselect the **Original Configuration** check box.

10. Click the **OK** button.

11. Click the **Close** button.

12. Click the **Start** button.

13. Select the **Shut Down** option and restart the lab workstation.

Student 2

1. After Student 1 has reconfigured the lab workstation, answer the following questions and repair the lab workstation. To repair your lab workstation you must be able to create and dial out using a dialer configured with the TCP/IP protocol to use the following DNS numbers:

Primary DNS: 15.8.457.1

Secondary DNS: 15.8.245.6

a. Are there any error messages? If so, write them down:

_____

_____

b. What is the problem (be specific)? _____

c. List several possible solutions: _____

d. Test your theory (solution) and record the results:

_____

_____

e. How did you discover the problem?

_____

_____

_____

f. What could you do differently next time to improve your troubleshooting process?

_____

_____

_____

_____

_____

_____

Troubleshooting modem communications in Windows NT

Student 2

The following steps should be performed while Student 1 is away from the lab workstation.

1. Power on the lab workstation and allow it to boot into Windows NT.

2. Log on into Windows NT.

3. Click the **Start** button.

4. Point to **Settings**.

5. Click **Control Panel**.

6. Double-click the **Network** icon.

7. Click the **Services** tab.

8. Double-click **Remote Access Service**.

9. Click the **Network** button.

10. Deselect the **TCP/IP** check box.

11. Select the **NetBeui** check box.

12. Click the **OK** button.

13. Click the **Continue** button.

14. If prompted, enter the path to the installation files.

15. Click the **Close** button.

16. Click the **Yes** button, and then restart the computer.

Student 1

1. After Student 2 has reconfigured the lab workstation, answer the following questions and repair the lab workstation. To repair your lab workstation, you must be able to create and dial out using a phone book entry with the TCP/IP protocol configured to use the following DNS numbers:

Primary DNS: 15.8.457.1

Secondary DNS: 15.8.245.6

a. Are there any error messages? If so, write them down:

_____

_____

b. What is the problem (be specific)? _____

c. List several possible solutions: _____

d. Test your theory (solution) and record the results:

_____

_____

e. How did you discover the problem?

_____

_____

_____

f. What could you do differently next time to improve your troubleshooting process?

_____

_____

_____

_____

_____

_____

Lab Notes

What is ISDN? – ISDN (acronym for Integrated Services Digital Network) is a communications standard that can carry digital data simultaneously over two channels on a single pair of wires at almost five times the speed of regular phone lines.

REVIEW QUESTIONS

Circle True or False.

1. RAS can be disabled via the Modems option in the Control Panel. True / False

2. Windows 95 will allow you to create multiple phone book entries. True / False

3. In Windows 95 you can view a modem's resources by using the Device Manager. True / False

4. In Windows NT you can view a modem's resources by using the Device Manager. True / False

5. Peggy wants to reinstall RAS on her Windows NT computer. Describe how Peggy could complete this task.

_____

_____

_____

_____

_____

6. Steve has decided to reinstall his modem driver on his Windows 95 computer. Describe the steps Steve should take to complete this task.

_____

_____

_____

_____

_____

15

NETWORKING FUNDAMENTALS AND THE INTERNET

LABS INCLUDED IN THIS CHAPTER

LAB 16.1 NETWORK COMPONENT IDENTIFICATION

LAB 16.2 NETWORKING AND WINDOWS 95

LAB 16.3 NETWORKING AND WINDOWS NT

LAB 16.4 USING THE INTERNET

Lab 16.1 Network Component Identification

Objective

The objective of this lab exercise is to allow you to install and configure a network interface card and to familiarize you with some of the common components of a networked environment. After completing this lab exercise, you will be able to:

- Install a network interface card.

- Identify some of the most commonly used networking components.

- Describe the functions of commonly used networking components.

Materials Required

This lab exercise requires one complete lab workstation for every four students. The lab workstations should meet the following requirements:

- 486 or better
- 8MB of RAM
- Windows 95

One network interface card for each lab workstation

This lab exercise also requires the following materials:

- DB-9 cable
- DB-25 cable
- One standard Centronics parallel cable
- RJ-25
- RJ-11
- RJ-14
- RJ-45
- BNC
- BNCT
- PS2/MINI-DIN
- ThickNet
- Unshielded twisted pair wire
- Shielded twisted pair wire
- One network interface card designed for use with both an RJ-45 connector and a BNC connector

If available for demonstration purposes, the instructor will need the following:

- One hub
- One router
- One switch
- Fiber optic cable and connectors

Any of the following networking devices:

- Network sniffer
- Protocol analyzer
- Time domain reflector
- Any type of ISDN devices

Lab Setup & Safety Tips

- The instructor should label each of the network and wiring components.
- Students should follow grounding and ESD procedures.
- Always unplug the system unit before touching components in the case.

ACTIVITY

Identifying network components

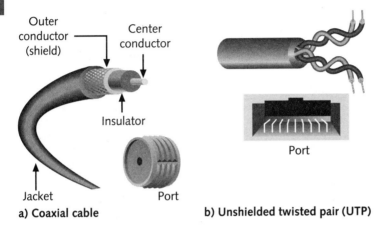

a) Coaxial cable

b) Unshielded twisted pair (UTP)

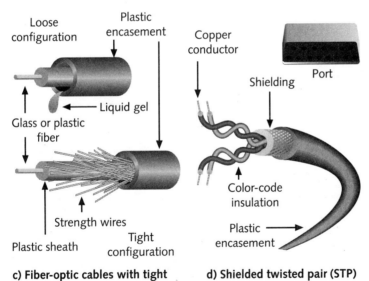

c) Fiber-optic cables with tight and loose sheaths

d) Shielded twisted pair (STP)

Figure 16-1   Networking cables

16

1. Describe the function of each of the following components, and explain how it could be used in a networked environment.

   a. DB-9 cable

   _____

   _____

   _____

   b. DB-25 cable

   _____

   _____

   _____

   c. Centronics parallel data cable

   _____

   _____

   _____

   d. RJ-25

   _____

   _____

   _____

   e. RJ-11

   _____

   _____

   _____

   f. RJ-14

   _____

   _____

   _____

   g. RJ-45

   _____

   _____

   _____

   h. BNC

   _____

   _____

   _____

i. BNCT

_____

_____

_____

j. PS2/MINI-DIN

_____

_____

_____

k. ThickNet

_____

_____

_____

l. Unshielded twisted pair wire

_____

_____

_____

m. Shielded twisted pair wire

_____

_____

_____

n. Network interface card

_____

_____

_____

o. Hub

_____

_____

_____

p. Router

_____

_____

_____

q. Switch

_____

_____

_____

16

r. Fiber optics

_____

_____

_____

s. Network sniffer

_____

_____

_____

t. Protocol analyzer

_____

_____

_____

u. Time domain reflector

_____

_____

_____

v. ISDN devices

_____

_____

_____

Installing the network interface card

1. Unplug the power cord.

2. Remove the case.

3. Locate an available slot where you plan to install the network interface card.

4. Using the provided documentation, verify that the network interface card is configured to use the predetermined I/O address and an available IRQ.

5. Gently install the network interface card into the slot. Warning: Don't bend the card from side to side; only move the card back and forth from end to end.

6. Screw the mounting screw into place.

7. Replace the top of the case.

8. Plug in the system unit.

9. Power on the lab workstation and allow it to boot into Windows 95.

10. If the workstation fails to boot properly, power cycle the PC, and when prompted, choose Safe Mode.

Lab Notes

What does RJ stand for? – RJ stands for registered jack.

What does LAN stand for? – The term LAN stand for local area network. This term is normally used to refer to a small or mid-sized network that is contained within a small geographical area.

What does WAN stand for? – The term WAN stands for wide area network. This term is normally used to refer to networks that are spread across a large geographical area.

What is a MAN? – The term MAN stands for metropolitan area network. This term is normally used to refer to small or mid-sized networks that are contained within a metropolitan area.

CERTIFICATION OBJECTIVES

Table 16-1   Core A+ objectives

Objective	Chapters	Page Numbers
1.3 Identify available IRQs, DMA's, and I/O addresses and procedures for configuring them for device installation, including identifying switch and jumper settings. Content may include the following:		
Standard IRQ settings	3	123
Differences between jumpers and switches	2, 6	52, 263
Locating and setting switches/jumpers	2, 6, 8	52, 63, 263, 388, 403, 409
Network Cards	1	8-9
1.4 Identify common peripheral ports, associated cabling, and their connectors. Content may include the following:		
Cable types	1, 4, 5	3, 4, 12, 169-170, 243
Cable orientation	1	3, 4
Cable and connector location - internal/external	3, 5, 8	119, 242, 402
Serial versus parallel	8, 14	393, 732
Pin connections	8	394
Cable handling/routing	16	812
Examples of types of connectors:		
DB9	8	393-395
DB25	8	393-395, 401
RJ11	Lab Manual	N/A
RJ14	Lab Manual	N/A
RJ45	Lab Manual	N/A
PS2/MINI-DIN	4	175
5.3 Identify the types of printer connections and configurations. Content may include the following:		
Parallel	8	400
Serial	8, 14	732, 400
Network	16	819-821
7.1 Identify basic networking concepts, including how a network works. Content may include the following:		
Network Interface Cards	16	819-821, 840
Cabling - Twisted Pair, Coaxial, Fiber Optic	16	812
7.2 Identify procedures for swapping and configuring network interface cards.	16	840-842

16

REVIEW QUESTIONS

Circle True or False.

1. An RJ-11 connector is commonly used as telephone wire. True / False

2. RJ stands for registered jack. True / False

3. RJ-45 connectors are often used in a LAN environment. True / False

4. BNC connectors are most commonly used in when connecting UTP. True / False

5. Describe the difference between UTP and STP.

   _____

   _____

   _____

   _____

   _____

6. Describe the difference between a router and a hub.

   _____

   _____

   _____

   _____

   _____

LAB 16.2 NETWORKING AND WINDOWS 95

OBJECTIVE

The objective of this lab exercise is to allow you hands-on networking experience in the Windows 95 environment. After completing this lab exercise, you will be able to:

- Install network interface card drivers.
- Configure Windows 95 to communicate on a LAN.
- Share resources in a networked environment.
- Map a network drive.
- Configure the TCP/IP protocol in the Windows 95 environment.

Materials Required

This lab exercise requires one complete lab workstation for every four students. The lab workstations should meet the following requirements:

- 486 or better
- 8MB of RAM
- Windows 95
- One network interface card

Lab Setup & Safety Tips

- Each lab workstation should have Windows 95 installed and functioning properly.
- Each lab workstation should have one network interface card installed.
- The classroom should be wired for network communications.
- The instructor will provide an IP address for each lab workstation prior to beginning the activities. Note: All IP addresses issued should be on the same subnet unless the classroom supports other configurations.
- The instructor will provide computer names for each lab workstation prior to completing the activities.

16

ACTIVITY

Installing network interface card drivers

The following lab exercise assumes that your lab workstation is not configured with any sort of networking components. If your lab workstation has any networking components installed, remove them all, and reboot your system before proceeding.

1. Power on your lab workstation and allow it to boot into Windows 95.
2. Click the **Start** button.
3. Point to **Settings**.
4. Click **Control Panel**.
5. Double-click the **Network** icon.
6. Click the **Add** button.
7. Double-click **Client**.
8. Select **Microsoft** from the Manufacturer list.

9. Double-click the **Client for Microsoft Networks** option.

10. Select the NIC manufacturer from the Manufacturer list.

11. Double-click the correct NIC driver.

12. Click the **Add** button.

13. Double-click the **Protocol** option.

14. Select **Microsoft** from Manufacturer list.

15. Double-click the **TCP/IP** option.

16. Click the **Identification** tab.

17. Type the computer name specified by your instructor.

18. Click the **OK** button.

19. If prompted, enter the path to the installation files.

20. Click the **Yes** button when you are prompted to restart your computer.

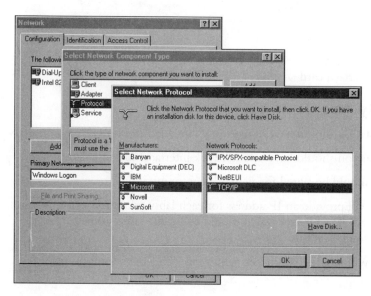

Figure 16-2   Installing TCP/IP for Windows 95 using the
Control Panel

Configuring the TCP/IP protocol

1. Click the **Start** button.

2. Point to **Settings**.

3. Click **Control Panel**.

4. Double-click the **Network** icon.

5. Double-click the **TCP/IP** protocol.

6. Click the **Specify an IP address** option button.

7. Type the IP address issued to your lab workstation.

8. Enter any additional information required by your instructor.

9. Click the **OK** button.

10. Click the **OK** button.

11. Click the **Yes** when prompted to restart your computer.

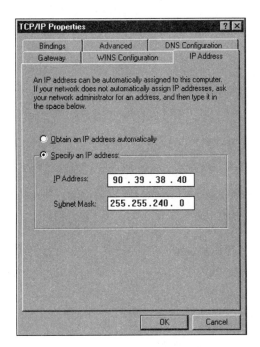

Figure 16-3   Configuring TCP/IP for Windows 95 static IP
addressing

Using the PING command the test the network

1. Click the **Start** button.

2. Point to **Programs**.

3. Click **MS–DOS Command Prompt**.

4. Type **PING** ###.###.###.### (### represents your lab workstation's IP address).

5. Type **PING** ###.###.###.### (### represents the IP address of your neighbor's lab workstation).

Enabling resource sharing

1. Click the **Start** button.

2. Point to **Settings**.

3. Click **Control Panel**.

4. Double-click the **Network** icon.

5. Click the **File and Printer Sharing** option button.

6. Place a check mark in both check boxes to allow the lab workstations to share resources.

7. Click the **OK** button.

8. Click the **OK** button.

9. Click the **Yes** when prompted to restart your computer.

Sharing your C drive

1. Double-click the **My Computer** icon.

2. Right-click the icon for your C drive.

3. Select **Properties** from the menu.

4. Click the **Sharing** tab.

16

5. Click the **Shared As** option button.

6. Click the **Full** option button.

7. Click the **OK** button.

Connecting to a shared resource

1. Right-click the **Network Neighborhood** icon.

2. Select the **Map Network Drive** option.

3. Use the drop-down arrow and choose the drive letter **G.**

4. Type **\\COMPUTERNAME\SHARENAME** in the path box (the computer and share name should be your neighbor's).

5. Click the **OK** button.

Lab Notes

What is a protocol? – A protocol is a language used by computers to communicate in an networked environment.

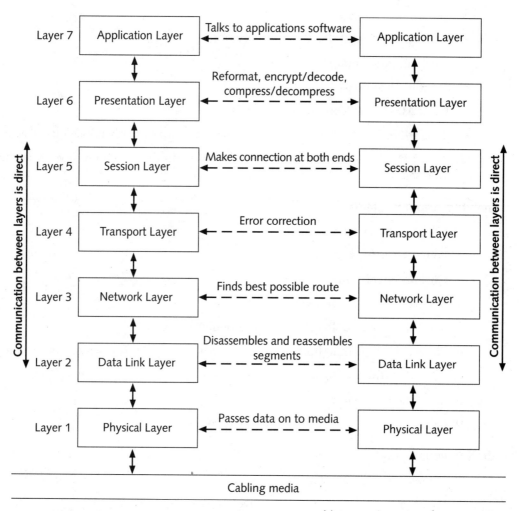

Figure 16-4   The OSI reference model identifies seven layers of network communication within software and firmware

What is bandwidth? – In the networking environment the term bandwidth refers to the amount of data that can travel through a wire at anyone time.

What is a gateway? - A gateway is a device or process that connects networks with different protocols. Often a router is used as a gateway.

What is DNS? – DNS stands for Domain Name System or Domain Name Service. DNS is a database on a top-level domain name server that keeps track of assigned domain names and their corresponding IP addresses.

CERTIFICATION OBJECTIVES

Table 16-2   DOS/Windows A+ objectives

Objective	Chapters	Page Numbers
5.1 Identify the networking capabilities of DOS and Windows including procedures for connecting to the network. Content may include the following:		
Sharing disk drives	16	875
Sharing print and file services	16	872, 880
Installing software	16	827
Network type and network card	16	810, 840
7.1 Identify basic networking concepts, including how a network works. Content may include the following:		
Protocol	16	828-832, 850
Ways to network a PC	16	830, 832, 838
7.3 Identify ramifications of repairs on the network. Content may include the following:		
Reduced bandwidth	16, App. E	843, E21
Loss of data	16, App. E	883, E22
Network slowdown	16	865

16

REVIEW QUESTIONS

Circle True or False.

1. You can configure Windows 95 to use an IP address via the Control Panel Network option. True / False

2. The ping command can be used to share network resources. True / False

3. All network drives that map from a Windows 95 PC to a Windows 95 PC must be mapped as drive G. True / False

4. Melanie can access her network properties on her Windows 95 computer by right-clicking on the My Computer icon and selecting the Properties option for the menu. True / False

5. Roy wants to enable file and printer sharing on his Windows 95 laptop. He has already installed TCP/IP and is able to ping on the network but he can't seem to share any files. Describe the steps that Roy should follow to in order to enable file and printer sharing.

_____

_____

_____

_____

_____

6. Where do you specify a computer and workgroup name in Windows 95?

_____

_____

_____

_____

_____

LAB 16.3 NETWORKING AND WINDOWS NT

OBJECTIVE

The objective of this lab exercise is to allow you hands-on networking experience in the Windows NT environment. After completing this lab exercise, you will be able to:

- Install network interface card drivers.
- Configure Windows NT workstation to communicate on a LAN.
- Share resources in a networked environment.
- Map a network drive in the Windows NT environment.
- Configure the TCP/IP protocol in the Windows NT environment.

Materials Required

This lab exercise requires one complete lab workstation for every four students. The lab workstations should meet the following requirements:

- 486 or better
- 16MB of RAM
- Windows NT
- One Network Interface card (must be NT compatible)

Lab Setup & Safety Tips

- The classroom should be wired for network communications.
- Each lab workstation should have Windows NT installed and functioning properly.
- Each lab workstation should have one network interface card installed.
- The instructor will provide an IP addresses for each lab workstation prior to beginning the activities. Note: All IP addresses issued should be on the same subnet unless the classroom supports other configurations.
- The instructor will provide computer names to each lab workstation prior to completing the activities.

16

ACTIVITY

Installing network interface card drivers and configuring TCP/IP

1. Power on your lab workstation and allow it to boot into the Windows NT environment.
2. Click the **Start** button.
3. Point to **Settings**.
4. Click **Control Panel**.
5. Double-click the **Network** icon.
6. Click the **Adapter** tab.
7. Click the **Add** button.
8. Select the correct NIC driver from the list provided.
9. Click the **OK** button.
10. If prompted, enter the path to the installation files.
11. Click the **Protocol** tab.

12. Click the **Add** button.

13. Select **TCP/IP Protocol** from the list provided.

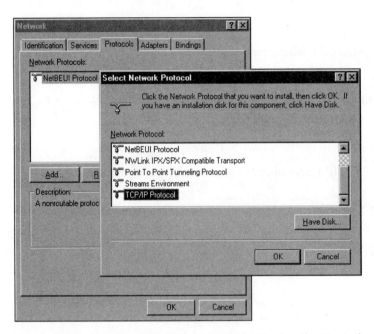

Figure 16-5 Installing TCP/IP for Windows NT using the Control Panel

14. Click the **OK** button.

15. Click the **Close** button.

16. Click the **No** button.

17. Type the IP addressed issued to your lab workstation.

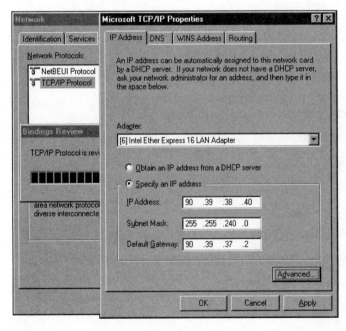

Figure 16-6 Configuring TCP/IP for Windows NT for static IP addressing

18. Enter any additional information required by your instructor.

19. Click the **OK** button.

20. Click the **Yes** button when prompted to restart your computer.

Using the PING command to test the network

1. Click on the **Start** button.

2. Point to **Programs**.

3. Click **MS-DOS Command Prompt**.

4. Type **PING** ###.###.###.### (### represents your lab workstation's IP address).

5. Type **PING** ###.###.###.### (### represents represents the IP address of your neighbor's lab workstation).

Sharing your C drive

1. Double-click the **My Computer** icon.

2. Right-click the icon for your C drive.

3. Select **Properties** from the menu.

4. Click the **Sharing** tab.

5. Click the **Not Shared** option button.

6. Click the **Apply** button.

7. Click the **Shared As** option button.

8. Click the **OK** button.

Connecting to a shared resource

1. Right-click the **Network Neighborhood** icon.

2. Select the **Map Network Drive** option.

3. Use the drop-down arrow and choose the drive letter **G.**

4. Type **\\COMPUTERNAME\SHARENAME** in the path box (the computer and share name should be your neighbor's).

5. Click the **OK** button.

16

Lab Notes

How is the default gateway used? – The default gateway is a gateway that a client will send its data packets through that are destined for an IP address on different network.

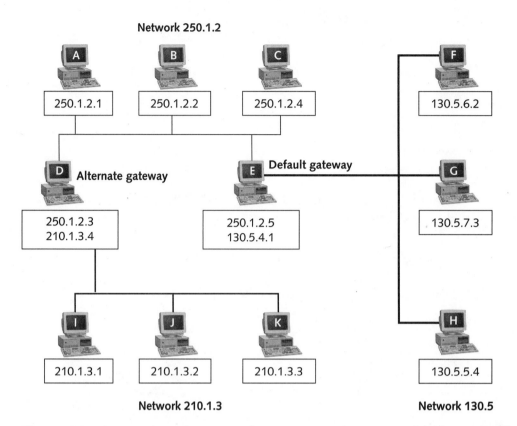

Figure 16-7   A network can have more than one router. One router of the network will be the default gateway

REVIEW QUESTIONS

Circle True or False.

1. Windows NT does not allow you to share your C drive. True / False

2. The PING command serves the same function in both Windows 95 and Windows NT. True / False

3. To install a protocol in the Windows NT environment, you must view the Network properties, choose the Protocol tab, and click the Add button. True / False

4. Roxy has decided to change her Windows NT computer name. In order to complete this task, Roxy should open the Network properties window and choose the Bindings tab. True / False

5. Windows NT allows you to share and connect to different network resources. True / False

6. Max wants to connect his Windows NT computer to a UNIX share. Max wants the UNIX share to appear as drive N in his My Computer window. Describe the steps Max needs to follow in order to map a UNIX share as his network drive N.

_____

_____

_____

_____

_____

LAB 16.4 USING THE INTERNET

OBJECTIVE

The objective of this lab exercise is to allow you to develop your Internet skills. These skills include the installation and configuration of Internet software, as well as the browsing and downloading of information from the Internet. After completing this lab exercise, you will be able to:

- Install Netscape Communicator 4.04.
- Configure a Netscape profile.
- Use the HTTP protocol to connect and view Web sites.
- Use the FTP protocol to download files from an FTP site.

Materials Required

This lab exercise requires one complete lab workstation for every four students. The lab workstations should meet the following requirements:

- 486 or better
- 8MB of RAM
- Windows 95
- One modem

Netscape Communicator 4.04 standard edition or later

Lab Setup & Safety Tips

- Each lab workstation should have access to the Internet and Windows 95 installed and functioning properly.
- Each lab workstation should have the Netscape Communicator installation files on drive C prior the beginning the activity.

ACTIVITY

Installing Netscape Communicator 4.04 standard edition

1. Power on your lab workstation and allow it to boot into Windows 95.
2. Double-click the Netscape button in the **Setup** program icon.
3. Click the **Yes** button.
4. Click the **Next** button.
5. Click the **Yes** button.
6. Click the **Next** button.
7. Click the **Yes** button.
8. Click the **Next** button.
9. Click the **Install** button.
10. Click the **No** button.
11. Click the **OK** button.
12. Click the **OK** button to restart your computer.

16

Configuring your Netscape profile

1. Click the **Start** button.

2. Point to **Programs**.

3. Click **Netscape Communicator**.

4. Click the **Netscape Messenger** icon.

5. Click the **Next** button.

6. Type your name in the Full Name box.

7. Type your e-mail address in the Email address box.

8. Click the **Next** button.

9. Type your name in the Profile Name box.

10. Click the **Next** button.

11. Type the name of you SMTP server in the Outgoing Mail (SMTP) Server box.

12. Click the **Next** button.

13. Type your mail server user name in the Mail Server User Name box.

14. Type the name of your POP or IMAP sever in the Incoming Mail Server box.

15. Click the correct option button to specify either a POP3 sever or an IMAP server.

16. Click the **Next** button.

17. Type the name of your news server in the **News (NNTP) server** box.

18. Click the **Finish** button.

19. Click the **Do not perform this check in the future** check box to select it.

20. Click the **Yes** button.

21. Close the Netscape Messenger.

Using the HTTP protocol

1. If necessary, connect to the Internet.

2. Launch the Netscape Communicator.

3. In the location box, type WWW.MICROSOFT.COM.

4. Press **Enter**.

Using the FTP protocol

1. Launch the Netscape Communicator.

2. In the location box, type ftp://ftp.microsoft.com.

3. After you are connected to the Microsoft FTP site, browse to the following directory: ftp://ftp.microsoft.com/Services/TechNet/UPM/ (UPM stands for Ultimate Printer Manual).

4. Download the Ultimate Printer Manual by clicking on the link called UPM.EXE.

5. Click the **Save** button.

   (This process will take some time - the UPM.EXE file is several megabytes.)

Configuring Netscape Communicator browser to use a proxy server

In the following section you will configure your Web browser to use to use a sample proxy server for the HTTP and FTP services called WEB-PROXY.LAB.TEST.COM:8088.

1. Launch the Netscape Communicator.
2. Click the **Edit** menu.
3. Select **Preferences** from the menu.
4. In the Category, double-click the **Advanced** option.
5. Click **Proxies**.
6. Click the **Manual Proxy configuration** option button.
7. Click the **View** button.
8. In the HTTP box, type **WEB-PROXY.LAB.TEST.COM**, press Tab and type **8088**.
9. In the FTP box, type **WEB-PROXY.LAB.TEST.COM**, press Tab and type **8088**.
10. Click the **OK** button.
11. Click the **OK** button.

CERTIFICATION OBJECTIVES

Table 16-3   DOS/Windows A+ objectives

Objective	Chapters	Page Numbers
5.2 Identify concepts and capabilities relating to the Internet and basic procedures for setting up a system for Internet access. Content may include the following:		
Downloading	16	872
E-mail	16	870
HTML	16	871
HTTP://	16	871
FTP	16	872-873
Domain Names (Web sites)	16	872
ISP	16	849
Configuring browser	16	870
E-mail set up	16	870

16

Lab Notes

What is an ISP? – ISP stands for Internet service provider. ISPs are used as connection points to the Internet. From home most people will dial into an ISP's network that is connected to the Internet. This allows the home user access to the Internet.

REVIEW QUESTIONS

Circle True or False.

1. Netscape Communicator is a Web server software package. True / False
2. The HTTP protocol is used when viewing Web pages like www.microsoft.com. True / False
3. You can download by simply clicking on the link to the file and pressing the Save button. True / False

4. Netscape Communicator does not support proxy servers. True / False

5. Describe the steps necessary to connect to an FTP site.

_____

_____

_____

_____

_____

6. List three examples of domain names.

_____

_____

_____

_____

_____

Viruses, Disaster Recovery, and a Maintenance Plan That Works

LABS INCLUDED IN THIS CHAPTER

LAB 17.1 VIRUS PROTECTION

LAB 17.2 CREATING AND MAINTAINING BACKUPS

LAB 17.3 DESIGNING A PREVENTATIVE MAINTENANCE PLAN

LAB 17.1 VIRUS PROTECTION

Objective

The objective of this lab exercise is to learn to identify virus symptoms and learn how to use antivirus software to detect and disinfect viruses. After completing this lab exercise, you will be able to:

- Scan for viruses using antivirus software.
- Name some of the most common types of viruses.
- Describe the effects of several different types of viruses.

Materials Required

This lab exercise requires one complete lab workstation for every two students. The lab workstation should meet the following requirements:

- 486 or better
- 8MB of RAM
- Windows 95
- Nuts & Bolts software
- Access to the Internet

Lab Setup & Safety Tips

- Each lab workstation should have Windows 95 installed and functioning properly.
- Each lab workstation should have the Cheyenne Antivirus software installed prior to beginning the activities.

ACTIVITY

Scanning for viruses

1. Power on your lab workstation and allow it to boot into Windows 95.
2. Click the **Start** button.
3. Point to **Programs**, then point to **Nuts & Bolts**.
4. Click **Cheyenne Antivirus Scanner**.
5. In the Scanning box, type **c:**.
6. Click **Advanced**.
7. Verify that both the Boot Sector and the Files options are selected.
8. Click the **File Types** tab.
9. Verify that the **All Files** option is selected.
10. Click the **OK** button.
11. Click the **Start** button.

Researching viruses and describing their symptoms

1. In the following section you will research viruses and their symptoms. In each of the following categories, list five different types of viruses and describe their symptoms. Use the Internet as a research tool. You will find information about viruses at each of the listed in the following table.

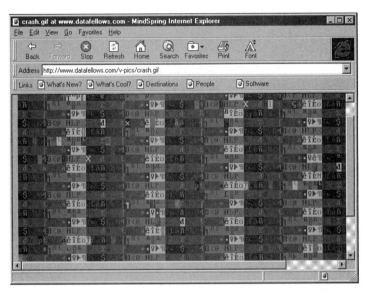

Figure 17-1 Crash virus (Screen displays garbage, but no damage is done to the hard drive data)

a. Boot sector viruses

_____

_____

_____

_____

_____

b. Worm

_____

_____

_____

_____

c. Trojan horse

_____

_____

_____

_____

_____

17

d. Macro viruses

_____

_____

_____

_____

_____

e. Multipartite viruses

_____

_____

_____

_____

_____

f. Stealth viruses

_____

_____

_____

_____

_____

g. Partition table viruses

_____

_____

_____

_____

_____

h. Virus hoaxes

_____

_____

_____

_____

_____

Lab Notes

Where do viruses come from? – All viruses are written by programmers. You can receive a virus through many different forms of communications, some examples include disks, file downloads and even Web sites.

CERTIFICATION OBJECTIVES

Table 17-1   DOS/Windows A+ objectives

Objective	Chapters	Page Numbers
4.8 Identify concepts relating to viruses and virus types - their danger, their symptoms, sources of viruses, how they infect, how to protect against them, and how to identify and remove them. Content may include the following:		
What they are	17	901-904
Sources	17	905
How to determine presence	17	908
Removal	17	907, 910
Prevention	17	907
Boot sector virus	17	902
FAT virus	17	909
Memory virus	17	909
Macro virus	17	903
CMOS virus	17	902

REVIEW QUESTIONS

Circle True or False.

1. All viruses can cause fatal damage to your operating system. True / False

2. If your PC freezes often you probably have a virus. True / False

3. Some viruses are designed to infect specific types of files such as Word 97 or Excel 97 documents. True / False

4. Currently there are 500 viruses in existence. True / False

5. Name three common ways viruses are contracted.

   _____

   _____

   _____

   _____

   _____

6. List two things you can do to help prevent the spread of viruses.

   _____

   _____

   _____

   _____

   _____

17

LAB 17.2 CREATING AND MAINTAINING BACKUPS

Objective

The objective of this lab exercise is to allow you the hands-on experience necessary to properly install, configure, and execute a full backup in the Windows NT environment. After completing this lab exercise, you will be able to:

- Install an external tape backup device.
- Configure Windows NT workstation to use an external tape backup device.
- Use the Windows NT backup program.

Materials Required

This lab exercise requires one complete lab workstation for every four students. The lab workstations should meet the following requirements:

- 486 or better
- 16MB of RAM
- Windows NT

One external tape backup drive

One tape for the backup drive

Lab Setup & Safety Tips

- Each lab workstation should have Windows NT installed and functioning properly.
- Each lab workstation should have one network interface card installed.
- Students must follow standard ESD procedures when handling hardware.
- Always unplug the system unit before touching components inside the case.
- Students should have the documentation and drivers necessary to install and configure the tape backup drive.

ACTIVITY

Installing a tape backup drive

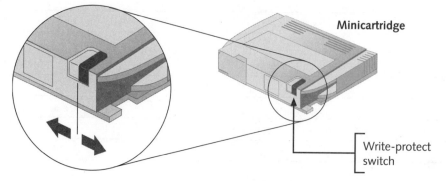

Figure 17-2   Minicartridge for a tape drive with write-protect switch

1. Power off your lab workstation.

2. Plug the parallel cable into the back of the tape drive.

3. Now attach the parallel cable to the LPT1.

4. Plug in and power on the tape drive.

5. Power on your lab workstation and allow it to boot into Windows NT.

Installing the tape backup drive's device drivers

1. Click the **Start** button.

2. Point to **Settings** and click **Control Panel.**

3. Double-click the **Tape Devices** icon.

4. Click the **Drivers** tab.

5. Click the **Add** button.

6. Insert the disk containing the tape drive device drivers.

7. Click the **Have Disk** button.

8. Click the **OK** button.

9. Select the correct drivers for your tape drive.

10. Click the **OK** button.

11. If prompted, enter the path to the Windows NT installation files.

12. Click the **Close** button.

13. Click the **Yes** button to restart your computer.

Using the Windows NT backup program

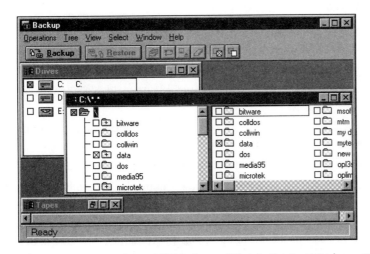

Figure 17-3   Windows NT backup utility similar to Windows 95 backup

1. Insert a tape into the tape backup drive.

2. Click the **Start** button.

3. Point to **Programs**.

4. Click **Administrative Tools**.

5. Click the **Backup** option.

6. In the Backup program window, click the **Operations** menu.

7. Select the **Hardware Setup** option.

8. Verify that the proper tape backup device is shown in the Hardware Setup box.

9. Click the **OK** button.

10. Place a check mark in the box next to the C: drive.

11. Click the **Operations** menu.

12. Choose **Backup**.

Lab Notes

What is a differential backup? – A differential backup only backs up files that have changed or have been created since the last full backup.

What is an incremental backup? – An incremental back only backs up files that have been changed or files that have been created since the last incremental or full backup.

CERTIFICATION OBJECTIVES

Table 17-2   DOS/Windows A+ objective

Objective	Chapters	Page Numbers
1.5 Identify the procedures for basic disk management. Content may include the following:		
Using disk management utilities	6	277-289
Backing up	4, 5, 6, 7	165, 233, 272, 368
Formatting	4, 5, 7	146, 151, 165, 220, 338

REVIEW QUESTIONS

Circle True or False.

1. The Windows NT backup program will allow you to backup files to either a floppy drive or a tape drive. True / False

2. You can install a tape drive device driver via the Control Panel Add New Hardware icon. True/ False

3. To begin a backup using the Windows NT backup program, launch the backup program and click the Tools menu and then click Backup Now. True / False

4. Windows NT supports full, incremental, and differential backups. True / False

5. The Windows NT backup program will automatically backup the PC nightly unless specified otherwise. True / False

6. Joy has decided to backup her hard drive. Joy understands how to execute the backup process but is unsure what kind of backup she should perform (incremental, differential, or full). Explain below which type of backup Joy must use and why.

_____

_____

_____

_____

LAB 17.3 DESIGNING A PREVENTATIVE MAINTENANCE PLAN

Objective

The objective of this lab exercise is to allow you the opportunity to create a preventative maintenance plan for a small business network. After completing this lab exercise, you will be able to:

- Design a preventative maintenance plan.
- Name some common preventative maintenance tasks for networked computers.
- Understand and describe the importance of maintenance delegation.

Materials Required

You will not require any additional materials for this exercise.

Lab Setup & Safety Tips

- Your instructor will discuss some of the more commonly used preventative maintenance procedures.

ACTIVITY

Developing a PC preventive maintenance plan

Table 17-3   Guidelines for developing a PC preventive maintenance plan

Component	Maintenance	How Often
Inside the case	■ Make sure air vents are clear. ■ Use compressed air to blow the dust out of the case. ■ Ensure that chips and expansion cards are firmly seated. ■ Clean the contacts on expansion cards.	Yearly
CMOS setup	■ Keep a backup record of setup (for example, use Nuts & Bolts rescue disk).	Whenever changes are made
Floppy drive	■ Only clean the floppy drive head when the drive does not work.	When the drive fails
Hard drive	■ Perform regular backups. ■ Automatically execute a virus scan program at startup. ■ Defragment the drive and recover lost clusters regularly. ■ Don't allow smoking around the PC. ■ Place the PC where it will not get kicked or bumped.	At least weekly At least daily Monthly
Keyboard	■ Keep the keyboard clean. ■ Keep the keyboard away from liquids.	Monthly Always
Mouse	■ Clean the mouse rollers and ball (see Chapter 7).	Monthly
Monitor	■ Clean the screen with a soft cloth.	At least monthly
Printers	■ Clean out the dust and bits of paper. ■ Clean the paper and ribbon paths with a soft cloth. ■ Don't re-ink ribbons or use recharged toner cartridges.	At least monthly

17

Table 17-3 Guidelines for developing a PC preventive maintenance plan (continued)

Component	Maintenance	How Often
Software	▪ If so directed by your employer, check that only authorized software is present. ▪ Regularly remove files from the Recycle Bin and \Temp directories. ▪ Remove any temporary files in the /DOS directory.	At least monthly
Written record	▪ Record all software, including version numbers and the OS installed on the PC. ▪ Record all hardware components installed, including hardware settings. ▪ Record when and what preventive maintenance is performed. ▪ Record any repairs done to the PC.	Whenever changes are made

1. You are the network administrator for a 75-user network. Your employer has asked you to create a preventive maintenance plan for all of the hardware components connected to the network. You have started this project by creating the following list, which contains each of the hardware components that should be included in the preventative maintenance plan. Using the table above for reference, write at least two preventive maintenance tasks for each of the listed hardware components. Be sure to state how often the preventive maintenance task should be completed and who should be responsible for completing the tasks (i.e. yourself or the user). Remember that you are the only network administrator and will not be able to realistically complete every preventative maintenance task necessary to maintain a network of this size.

    a. **System unit**

       i. PM Task 1

       _____

       _____

       _____

       ii. PM Task 2

       _____

       _____

       _____

    b. **CMOS setup**

       i. PM Task 1

       _____

       _____

       _____

       ii. PM Task 2

       _____

       _____

       _____

    c. **Floppy drive**

       i. PM Task 1

       _____

       _____

       _____

    ii. PM Task 2

_____

_____

_____

  d. **Hard drive**

    i. PM Task 1

_____

_____

_____

    ii. PM Task 2

_____

_____

_____

  e. **Keyboard and mouse**

    i. PM Task 1

_____

_____

_____

    ii. PM Task 2

_____

_____

_____

  f. **Monitors**

    i. PM Task 1

_____

_____

_____

    ii. PM Task 2

_____

_____

_____

  g. **10 Laser printers**

    i. PM Task 1

_____

_____

_____

    ii. PM Task 2

_____

_____

_____

17

h. **7 Inkjet printers**

  i. PM Task 1

  _____

  _____

  _____

  ii. PM Task 2

  _____

  _____

  _____

Lab Notes

What is a PM kit? – PM kits or preventative maintenance kits are designed to keep printers in good working order. Normally a PM kit is administered during off-business hours and is used to simply refresh and revitalize printer components that receive the most wear.

CERTIFICATION OBJECTIVES

Table 17-4 Core A+ Objectives

Objective	Chapters	Page Numbers
3.1 Identify the purpose of various types of preventive maintenance products and procedures, and when to use/perform them. Content may include the following:		
Liquid cleaning compounds	4	181
Types of materials to clean contacts and connections	4, 17	181, 899
Types of tools used for cleaning floppy drives: head cleaning disk	App. E	E3
Manufacturer guidelines	17	898, 899
Observations/identify wear and tear to determine need for maintenance.	17	899
Vacuum out systems, power supplies, fans	17, App. E	899, E15
Industry standards, normal use versus heavy use or environmental considerations	Student Workbook	N/A

REVIEW QUESTIONS

Circle True or False

1. Tasks in a preventive maintenance plan must be completed only by the network administrator. True / False

2. PM kits are normally designed to minimize printer downtime. True / False

3. Shaking the dust out of a system unit is considered an excellent preventative maintenance task that should be completed once a month. True / False

4. Smoking around a hard drive can shorten the length of its life. True / False

5. If all of the client computers are using the Windows NT operating system, you will not need to create a preventive maintenance program. True / False

CHAPTER EIGHTEEN

THE PROFESSIONAL PC TECHNICIAN

LABS INCLUDED IN THIS CHAPTER

LAB 18.1 TELEPHONE SUPPORT

LAB 18.2 ON-SITE SUPPORT

LAB 18.3 DOCUMENTING YOUR WORK

LAB 18.1 TELEPHONE SUPPORT

Objective

The objective of this lab exercise is to allow you to simulate a technical support call. After completing this lab exercise, you will be able to:

- Troubleshoot both hardware and software problems over the phone.

- Describe the advantages and disadvantages of supporting PCs over the phone.

- Understand the importance of listening to your customer.

Materials Required

This lab exercise requires one complete lab workstation for every two students. The lab workstations should meet the following requirements:

- 486 or better
- 8MB of RAM
- Windows 95
- One modem

Lab Setup & Safety Tips

- The modem should be installed and functioning properly prior to beginning the activity.

- During this lab exercise you will be simulating a telephone support call. For the most realistic results the student in the role of the technician should not be able to see what his or her customer is doing on the lab workstation.

- If students are working in pairs, assign Student 1 and Student 2.

ACTIVITY

Student 2 (Customer)

In this activity, you will delete the currently installed modem. Then, after restarting your computer, you will call your customer support line.

1. Power on your lab workstation and allow it to boot into Windows 95.

2. Right-click the **My Computer** icon.

3. Select **Properties** from the menu.

4. Click the **Device Manager** tab.

5. Double-click **Modems**.

6. Select the installed modem and press the **Delete** key.

7. Click the **Close** button.

8. Click the **Yes** button when prompted to restart your computer.

9. Call the customer support line, and explain that you have installed a modem but can't make it dial.

Student 1 (Technician)

The only resources you should have during this simulation is a pen and a piece of paper. After providing telephone support to your customer, answer the following questions.

Were there any error messages? If so, write them down:

_____

_____

_____

What was the problem?

_____

_____

List several (about three) clues that helped lead you to the problem (include what the customer said):

_____

_____

_____

_____

_____

What could you do differently next time to improve your troubleshooting process?

_____

_____

_____

_____

_____

Student 1 (Customer)

You are calling customer support (Student 2) because you want to install some memory that you have recently purchased but are not sure how to install it.

1. Power off your lab workstation and unplug it.

2. Remove the case.

3. Remove all of the RAM.

4. Call the customer support line, and explain that you have removed the case and want to install your new memory (use the memory you removed as the new memory for this exercise).

18

Student 2 (Technician)

The only resources you should have during this simulation is a pen and a piece of paper. After providing telephone support to your customer, answer the following questions:

Were there any error messages? If so, write them down:

_____

_____

_____

What was the problem?

_____

_____

_____

List several (about three) clues that helped lead you to the problem (include customer dialog):

_____

_____

_____

_____

What could you do differently next time to improve your troubleshooting process?

_____

_____

_____

_____

_____

Lab Notes

Listening to your customers – While working through this lab exercise, you probably discovered the importance of listening to your customer. You will find that at the beginning of a support call it is a good idea to allow your customer to explain his or her problem in detail and allow the customer to explain each step that he or she has taken prior to their call. A good technician listens to the customer and at times allows the customer to troubleshoot the problem. Some customers will already know the answer to their problem, but lack the confidence to follow through.

Maintaining control of a call – Although it is important to listen to your customers, don't lose control of the conversation or situation. If you feel you are beginning to lose control, ask your customer any questions that you may need answered and then reiterate what they have said to you. At this point explain to the customer what the next step to resolving their problem will be and make sure that this is acceptable.

CERTIFICATION OBJECTIVES

Table 18-1   Core A+ objectives

Objective	Chapters	Page Numbers
2.2 Identify basic troubleshooting procedures and good practices for eliciting problem symptoms from customers. Content may include the following:		
Troubleshooting/isolation /problem determination procedures	7	345
Determine whether hardware or software problem	7	349
Gather information from user regarding, e.g., Customer Environment	7, 18	347, 946
8.1 Differentiate effective from ineffective behaviors as these contribute to the maintenance or achievement of customer satisfaction. Some of the customer satisfaction behaviors and factors addressed include:		
Communicating and listening (face-to-face or over the phone)	18	949
Interpreting verbal and nonverbal cues	18	950
Responding appropriately to the customer's technical level	18	951
Establishing personal rapport with the customer	18	950
Professional conduct	18	951
Conflict avoidance and resolution	18	953

REVIEW QUESTIONS

Circle True or False.

1. As a technician you should always be sensitive to your customer's situation. True or False

2. Always tell your customers what to do. True or False

3. Customers can often provide clues to their problem. True or False

4. What do you think the three most important personality traits a help desk technician should have?

_____

_____

_____

_____

_____

18

LAB 18.2 ON-SITE SUPPORT

Objective

The objective of this lab exercise is to allow you to simulate a desktop PC support call. After completing this lab exercise you will be able to:

- Troubleshoot both hardware and software problems while communicating with a customer.
- Describe the advantages and disadvantages of desktop support.

Materials Required

This lab exercise requires one complete lab workstation for every two students. The lab workstation should meet the following requirements:
- 486 or better
- 8MB of RAM
- Windows 95

One DOS System Disk

Lab Setup & Safety Tips

- Each lab workstation should have Windows 95 installed and functioning properly.
- If students are working in pairs, assign Student 1 and Student 2.

ACTIVITY

Student 2 (Customer)

You have called a technician out to your desk because your system won't boot and is giving you the error message "Invalid or missing command interpreter: command.com". Complete the following steps while Student 1 is away from the lab workstation.

1. Insert a system disk in drive A.
2. Power on your lab workstation and allow it to boot from the system disk.
3. At the A prompt, type **C:** and press **Enter**.
4. Type **REN C:\COMMAND.COM C:\COMMAND.OLD**.
5. Press **Enter**.
6. Type **REN C:\MSDOS.SYS C:\MSDOS.OLD**.
7. Press **Enter**.
8. Reboot your lab workstation and verify that you receive the error message, "Invalid or missing command interpreter: command.com".
9. Ask your technical support person for help. Explain that you just installed some registry cleaning software and now nothing works right.

Student 1 (Technician)

The only resources you should have during this simulation is a pen and a piece of paper. After providing on-site support, answer the following questions:

Were there any error messages? If so, write them down:

_____

_____

_____

What was the problem?

_____

_____

_____

List several (about three) clues that helped lead you to the problem (include customer dialog):

_____

_____

_____

What could you do differently next time to improve your troubleshooting process?

_____

_____

_____

_____

Student 1 (Customer)

You will reposition the RAM so your system won't boot. Complete the following steps while Student 2 is away from the lab workstation.

1. Power off and unplug the lab workstation.
2. Remove the case.
3. Unplug the data cable to the hard drive.
4. Change the jumper to the Slave position.
5. Reposition the RAM and move it into the wrong banks.
6. Replace the case.
7. Power on the lab workstation and enter the setup program.
8. Remove the hard drive from the setup program.
9. Save the changes and exit.
10. Ask your technical support person for help. Explain that you didn't touch anything except for the memory because you just installed new memory.

Student 2 (Technician)

The only resources you should have during this simulation is a pen and a piece of paper. After providing on-site support, answer the following questions:

Were there any error messages? If so, write them down:

_____

_____

_____

What was the problem?

_____

_____

_____

18

List several three clues that helped lead you to the problem (include customer dialog):

_____

_____

_____

_____

What could you do differently next time to improve your troubleshooting process?

_____

_____

_____

_____

Lab Notes

Safe Mode – Safe Mode is a Windows 95 troubleshooting mode. When Windows 95 is started in Safe Mode, it will only load a minimal set of drivers that are necessary to load Windows. You can boot Windows 95 into Safe Mode by pressing the F8 key during the boot process.

CERTIFICATION OBJECTIVES

Table 18-2   Core A+ objectives

Objective	Chapters	Page Numbers
2.2 Identify basic troubleshooting procedures and good practices for eliciting problem symptoms from customers. Content may include the following:		
Troubleshooting/isolation /problem determination procedures	7	345
Determine whether hardware or software problem	7	349
Gather information from user regarding, e.g., Customer Environment	7, 18	347, 946
8.1 Differentiate effective from ineffective behaviors as these contribute to the maintenance or achievement of customer satisfaction. Some of the customer satisfaction behaviors and factors addressed include:		
Communicating and listening (face-to-face or over the phone)	18	949
Interpreting verbal and nonverbal cues	18	950
Responding appropriately to the customer's technical level	18	951
Establishing personal rapport with the customer	18	950
Professional conduct	18	951
Conflict avoidance and resolution	18	953

Table 18-3   DOS/Windows A+ objectives

Objective	Chapters	Page Numbers
4.1 Recognize and interpret the meaning of common error codes, startup messages, and icons from the boot sequence for DOS, Windows 3.x, and Windows 95. Content may include the following:		
Windows 95:		
Missing or corrupt Himem.sys	9	445
No operating system found	App. E	E4
Safe Mode	11	561
Bad or missing Command.com	6, App. E	322, E3
4.2 Identify the steps required to correct a startup or boot problem.	6	324, 338

REVIEW QUESTIONS

Circle True or False.

1. Safe Mode can be used to troubleshoot Windows 95. True or False

2. You can enter Safe mode by pressing the F8 key during the boot process. True or False

3. Windows 95 doesn't need the COMMAND.COM or MSDOS.SYS files. True or False

4. Troubleshooting the Windows NT environment is very similar to troubleshooting the Windows 95 environment. True or False

5. Describe how a Windows 95 repair disk can be used to repair the Windows 95 startup environment.

6. Lesa has decided to clean some files off of her hard drive but isn't sure if some of the files are safe to delete. Make Lesa a list of five files that she should not delete.

_____

_____

_____

_____

18

LAB 18.3 DOCUMENTING YOUR WORK

Objective

The objective of this lab exercise is to give you the opportunity to document your work from the previous lab exercises. After completing this lab exercise, you will be able to:

- Complete a standard service-call report form.
- Complete a standard help desk call report form.
- Describe the values of A+ certification.

Materials Required

You will not require any additional materials for this lab exercise.

Lab Setup & Safety Tips

- To complete the following activity you must have already completed Labs 8.1 and 8.2.

ACTIVITY

Documenting your help desk call (from Lab 8.1)

1. Complete the following Help Desk Report Form with the information from the activities in Lab 8.1.

Help Desk Call Report Form

Call

Caller:———————————— Date:———— Time:————
Location:———————————— Phone:————————
Received by:————————————
Description:————————————————————
————————————————————————

Notes on the Call

Follow-up Call on———————— **By** ————————

Follow-up Call on———————— **By** ————————

Outcome of Call

☐ Solved
☐ Unresolved

Figure 18-1   Help Desk Call Report Form

Documenting your PC support call (from Lab 8.2)

1. Complete the following Service Call Report Form with the information from the activities in Lab 8.2.

Service Call Report Form

Initial Request

Requested by:———————— Date:———— Time:————
Received by:———————— Phone 1:————
Phone 2:————
Description of problem:————————————————

Initial Action

Advice: _____
Appointment Made:
By: ———————— Date:———— Time:————————
Directions:————————————————

Source of Problem

———————————————————— ☐ Hardware
———————————————————— ☐ Software
———————————————————— ☐ User

Solution or Outcome

———————————————————— ☐ Repair
———————————————————— ☐ Replace
———————————————————— ☐ Educate
———————————————————— ☐ Other

Notes

————————————————————
————————————————————
————————————————————
————————————————————

Figure 18-2 Service Call Report Form

18

Lab Notes

What are the advantages of A+ certification? – A + certification is industry-recognized proof of competence and will greatly improve/increase your job opportunities.

What are your copyright responsibilities? – You are responsible for complying with the license agreement of the software package you are installing. It is also your responsibility to purchase only legitimate software packages that are properly licensed. You should report any software piracy issue by calling 1-888-NOPIRACY.

Other technical support resources

Table 18-4   Technical support Web sites

Web Site	Responsible Organization
www.aserve.net	Advanced Services Network
www.byte.com	BYTE Magazine
www.cnet.com	CNET.Inc.
www.cybercollege.com	CyberCollege
www.datafellows.com	Data Fellows Inc.
www.disktrend.com	DISK/TREND, Inc.
www.modems.com	Zoom Telephonics, Inc.
www.pc-today.com	PC Today Online
www.pcwebopedia.com	Sandy Bay Software, Inc.
www.pcworld.com	PC World
www.sangoma.com	Sangoma Technologies, Inc.
www.sysdoc.com	Tom's Hardware Guide
www.tcp.ca	The Computer Paper
www.windows95.com	Steve Jenkins and Jenesys, LLC.
www.zdnet.com	ZDNet

CERTIFICATION OBJECTIVES

A+

Table 18-5   Core A+ objectives

Objective	Chapters	Page Numbers
8.1 Differentiate effective from ineffective behaviors as these contribute to the maintenance or achievement of customer satisfaction. Some of the customer satisfaction behaviors and factors addressed include:		
Professional conduct	18	951

REVIEW QUESTIONS

Circle True or False.

1. Copyright protection is everyone's responsibility. True / False

2. One of your customers, John, asked you several weeks ago to create a shortcut to File Manager for him. He has now called you back in frustration because the shortcut you made has stopped working. Describe the best way to diffuse this situation.

   _____

   _____

   _____

   _____

3. List at least three reasons why call report forms are used.

   _____

   _____

   _____

4. Cindy has no previous experience working on a PC. To complete her job duties, she must be able to use Microsoft Word. List five or more things you would teach Cindy to help her be successful.

   _____

   _____

   _____

   _____